CONTEMPORARY
MOVIE
MONOLOGUES

MONOLOGUES FROM LITERATURE
A Sourcebook for Actors

Edited by Marisa Smith and Kristin Graham

CONTEMPORARY MOVIE MONOLOGUES

A Sourcebook for Actors

EDITED BY

MARISA SMITH

AND

JOCELYN BEARD

Fawcett Columbine
NEW YORK

Library of Congress Catalog Card Number: 90-82333

ISBN: 0-449-90354-0

Cover design by James R. Harris
Text design by Holly Johnson

Manufactured in the United States of America

First Edition: March 1991
10 9 8 7 6 5 4 3 2 1

CONTENTS

FOREWORD

Few aspects of the actor's experience create as much anxiety as the process of audition. Should I dress the part to show my rightness; should I dress against the part to show my range? Should I choose material twenty years beyond me in age and experience to show that I can stretch; should I grab the parts I've almost outgrown before they slip away from me altogether? The concern is always how to present oneself, but the trap for the actor is the excessive need to meet the expectations of the auditioner. Who is the actor really? What are the impulses, the instincts, that mark his or her uniqueness as an artist? The sense of self for all of us is fragile at best—for the actor, it may be gossamer as mist—yet it is the substance of all his or her best work.

So how can this book help? The essence of great film acting is its immediacy: What the camera photographs is thought in action. The best speeches from our favorite films, and this book has most of them, provide an arena for the actor's encounter with himself. The words become the avenue for an inner exploration and that journey can reveal all that is most particular, most specific, about an individual talent. Great screenwriters, and again all the finest are represented here, define the articulate by the careful detail of their language: The speeches in this book that are meant to convey the thoughts and feelings of highly verbal men and women do so by the economical selection of what is said. Thus, movie monologues may not always celebrate language for its own sake as much as classic stage writing, but that is not to suggest that the word itself is any less important.

Great movie monologues can provide the actor with still another vital opportunity; that of illuminating a character who is, in the core of his or her nature, *inarticulate*—passionate without easy expression. Speech after speech in this book presents the challenge of filling out the pauses, creating from the dots and dashes of hesitant speech a clear-cut and flowing emotional language. There is no hiding for the actor here; only his own being can transmit life where there is no verbal imagery to rely on.

And so these monologues, these beloved morsels from some of our most beloved movie meals, are profound exercises in the actor's craft. Whether used in the audition room or the classroom, on the stage or in the study, they will stretch muscles the actor might never know he had, yet never twist out of shape the actor's spirit, nor impede the search for the actor's own soul.

Arvin Brown
Artistic Director
Long Wharf Theatre

EDITOR'S INTRODUCTION

In the unending quest for the perfect audition monologue, the works of the world's great screenwriters provide an exciting and near-inexhaustible source. Master wordsmiths like Paul Schrader, Ray Bradbury, and Woody Allen have all lent their formidable talents to the silver screen, creating some of the most memorable moments in the history of the performing arts.

This book is offered to the auditioning actor and actress in the hope that among these pages you will find that most elusive perfect monologue. And so you are hereby invited to take a look within, but be warned: we've assembled some potent stuff! From the blistering (*Mississippi Burning*) to the romantic (*When Harry Met Sally*), every effort has been made to present a respectable variety of monologues from contemporary world cinema. All ages, sexes, and types of roles are equally represented; giving you, the performer, a wide assortment from which to choose.

While researching this book, we had no choice but to assign ourselves the task of watching most of these films at home. Imagine! Being forced to curl up on our comfy couches, pad and pencil in hand and having to sit through films like *The Days of Wine and Roses*, *Hannah and Her Sisters*, and *Anne of the Thousand Days* for hours on end! It was nothing short of . . . pure pleasure. We can only hope that you will enjoy using this book as much as we did putting it together. Enjoy, and Break a Leg!

HOW TO USE THIS BOOK

It's audition time! Okay, okay—don't panic. Take a deep breath and turn to the back of this book and behold with great relief the handy chart created for your browsing pleasure. You say you're a young kinda guy auditioning for a comedy role? No problem! Just flip right to the male section of the chart and take a gander! Women should try their luck in the female section. All roles are listed by age and type (comedy, serio-comedy, or drama.) With all the useful information offered on the chart, it's easier than ever to find the monologues that are right for you.

CONTEMPORARY
MOVIE
MONOLOGUES

BUTTERFIELD 8

1960

MGM & Alton Linebrook Productions
Screenplay by Charles Schnee and John Michael Hayes
Based on the novel by John O'Hara
Directed by Daniel Mann
Produced by Pandro S. Berman

3 MONOLOGUES
Gloria 1
Happy
Gloria 2

SETTING: New York City, early 1960s

Gloria is a gorgeous young woman with a knack for getting into trouble. A fashion model who hops from bed to bed, Gloria's wild nature and great beauty attract a seemingly endless procession of men.

One man, however, manages to break through Gloria's iron defenses: Liggot. A man living off his wife and her family, Liggot is a ruined shell of his former enterprising self. Once a successful and idealistic lawyer, Liggot has allowed his life to disintegrate until all he lives for is booze and sex. Gloria and Liggot connect like wildfire, and each is totally consumed with passion for the other. For the first time in her life, Gloria is truly in love, and Liggot finally sees a way out of his pit of despair.

Unfortunately, the lovers are never to realize happiness together. Liggot's wife discovers the affair, and Gloria flees the city, unable to reconcile her past with any hope for the future. Liggot chases after her, and watches in horror as she drives her car off a cliff. All but destroyed, Liggot returns to his wife to collect his things and to say goodbye. He blames himself for Gloria's death, and wishes to find absolution in the anonymity of a new life.

GLORIA 1

Here, Gloria tells her mother about her love for Liggot. She begs her mother to allow her to tell the truth about her life, and convinces her that her feelings for Liggot are genuine and have the power to redeem her sordid past.

Mama, I want to tell you what I've been doing. I do. I've been with a man a whole week. Let me tell you the truth for once in my life! Mama, we—we both know what kind of girl I've been. We both know what I've been doing. Mama, you have to! Unless I can be honest with you about yesterday, how can you believe me today? I'm different, Mama, I am different! Yesterday it was men—a whole world full of men. Mama, face it, I was the slut of all time. *(Her mother slaps her.)* If only you'd done that before—long ago, everytime I came home, all soaked through with gin. Oh, it's not your fault, Mama, it never has been. It was in me, but it isn't there any more. It's no longer just men for me—there's only one man. One, just one. Maybe it's too late for marriage, but it's not too late for love. Now, by some miracle, I'm like everybody else. I'm in love. You can look at me, Mama, without wishing I'd never been born.

HAPPY

The owner of the motel where Liggot and Gloria spent a night of passion speaks to a broken-hearted Gloria about her own past, and cautions Gloria not to end up as she has.

So, what was I saying? Oh, yeah. So she said to herself, you get in solid with the director—he'll put you in solid with the producer and pretty soon you'll wind up with a big part in the show. So, two days—

or should I say, two nights later, she was in solid, yeah, with the
director . . . with his cousin . . . she was so busy being in solid with
every Tom, Dick, and Harry and his Uncle George, she wouldn't
recognize a producer if she found one right under her pillow. You
take sugar? So, now time passes, and our heroine is very big, yeah,
but not in the theater. No, in all the wrong places. In five hundred
little black books; in twenty-eight divorce cases; two police blotters;
and in one restraining sheet in the psychopathic ward in Bellevue.
Yeah, she hit it big—from a size twelve dress to a size forty-four. She
went from looking like an orchid to a face like a pan of worms. And
all because she said, with only a rag, a bone, a hank of hair—I will
move the world my way! What's the matter? I'm boring you. Hey,
you live it up—you kick up your heels—you grab everything you
can—you light the candle from one end to the other, like they say.
And then, one day you too can be the proud proprietor of a very
heavily mortgaged roadside brothel, and wish you were dead.

GLORIA 2

*Gloria mistakenly thinks that Liggot despises her for having stolen his
wife's mink coat. Gloria goes to the apartment of Steve, her childhood
friend, and confesses the awful truth that she was molested as a child, and
how that has led to her life of sexual promiscuity.*

Steve, I have to tell you something. Nobody knows this except a
certain man somewhere who I like to think of as standing in the
middle of a lake filled with burning gasoline. Please listen. I was
thirteen, my father was dead. All older men seemed like fathers to
me, but I wanted one of my own—to sit in his lap, to hug him and
have him say I was beautiful. Do you remember Major Hartley? Major Hartley, my mother's friend. He came down to Grand Central
Station one day to pick me up from summer camp. Mother was away
visiting. He took me home. He let me sit on his lap. He let me hug
him. He told me I was beautiful. He stayed in that house for one
week, and taught me more about evil than any thirteen-year-old girl

in the world knew. You haven't heard the worst of it yet! I loved it! Every awful moment of it, I loved. That's your Gloria, Steve. That's your darling Gloria. I made a way of life out of it. The deep shame of it didn't hit me until it was too late. I couldn't go back to thirteen again. I had one chance to stop it. One last chance, and I threw it all away for thirty-two animals sewn together: the coat.

THE BIRD MAN OF ALCATRAZ

1962

United Artists
Screenplay by Guy Trosper
Based on the book by Thomas Gaddis
Directed by John Frankenheimer
Produced by Stuart Miller and Guy Trosper

2 MONOLOGUES
Gomez
Robert Stroud

SETTING: Leavenworth Prison, Alcatraz Prison, 1912–early 1960s

Robert Stroud was perhaps one of the most famous prison inmates in United States history. His crime when compared to others is rather unsensational; his incarceration, however, has attained the status of legend.

Stroud was sent to Leavenworth Prison in 1912 for killing a man in an argument. His hostile and antisocial behavior attracted the attention of Schumaker, the warden, who then went out of his way to make Stroud's imprisonment unpleasant. In an uncontrollable rage, Stroud killed a prison guard and was sentenced to die.

Stroud's devoted mother met with First Lady Edith Wilson and pleaded for the life of her son. Her efforts were rewarded when Stroud's sentence was commuted to life imprisonment in solitary confinement.

One day, as he was walking in the exercise yard, Stroud came upon a tiny bird with a broken wing. He rescued the bird and nursed it back to health in his cell. And so began his life's fascination and work. Before long, Stroud had managed to fill his cell with birds and scientific equipment with which to study them. He wrote volumes on their care, and even discovered cures for bird diseases. His writings and cures became nationally known, and soon the entire prison block was alive with birds.

Stroud's happiness was short-lived, however, for he was to be sent to the formidable rock of Alcatraz to live out his sentence. All of his books, equipment, and birds were taken away before he arrived in the grim fortress in San Francisco Bay. In Alcatraz, Stroud grew old. No longer the rage-filled man of his youth, his love for birds had helped to rehabilitate his nature. Stroud was finally released in the early 1960s, a quiet old man ready to live his own life.

GOMEZ

Robert Stroud's colorful death-row neighbor mourns the death of his bird, which Stroud has given him. The bird's death reminds him of a woman in his past.

Hey, Bob, you know, the baby bird just slipped me. Well, in case you're interested, he just knocked off. Punk. He dropped like he got shot in the head. Reminded me like an old girlfriend of mine named Peggy . . . Beaman. What a face! Like a pan-full of worms. But stacked—enough to make your tongue hang out. Good hearted broad, you know? She used to put out to me and every other guy in the neighborhood. A bum, in other words. Well, she had a bird, too. A parrot. And he, too, was ugly also—and one time I came up to her room and the door was open and she was trying to teach the parrot to say something. You'll get a boot out of this, Bob. You know what she wanted him to say? "I love you, Peggy." Over and over, you know? She kept at him: "I love you, Peggy." Oh, them two uglies. Figured she was some kind of nut so I faded and I never seen her no more after that time. Good old Peg. So what happens? So I wind up in the can and I'm talking to the birds just like she did.

ROBERT STROUD

The Bird Man releases the little sparrow who sparked his life's passion.
Stroud realizes that the bird was meant to fly free and forces it to leave
the prison cell through the bars in the window. As he urges the bird to
leave, he has bittersweet memories of freedom.

Springtime outside, Slugger. You best go find out who you are. What's
wrong with you—you old buzzard? Come on, don't be afraid. Out
there you can kick up the dust. You can dance to fiddle music; watch
the alfalfa bloom. If you like it you can see gold teeth taste sweet
whiskey or red-eyed gravy. The air breathes easy. The nights move
faster. You tell time on a clock. You don't want to be a jailbird all
your life, do you? You're a high-ballin' sparrow! So you fly high, old
cock. You go out there and bite the stars—for me. Find yourself a fat
mama and make a family, you hear? Beat it!

THE DAYS OF WINE AND ROSES

1962

Warner Brothers
A Martin Manulis Production
Screenplay by J.P. Miller
Directed by Blake Edwards
Produced by Martin Manulis

2 MONOLOGUES
Joe Clay
Kirstie Clay

SETTING: San Francisco, early 1960s

The Days of Wine and Roses is the tragic story of Joe and Kirstie Clay, a young married couple with almost everything going for them. Joe has a great job, they have a swell apartment, new baby, and a secure future. Unfortunately, Joe and Kirstie are both alcoholics, and their mutual addiction leads them over the edge of sanity into an abyss of rage and despair.

As Joe's drinking worsens, he is fired from job after job until he is no longer capable of presenting himself in the business world. At home, Kirstie does nothing but drink in front of the television, usually to the point of passing out, her baby daughter forgotten. On one such occasion, an untended cigarette starts a fire that destroys their apartment and everything they own.

Joe and Kirstie make several attempts to sober up, and in the process, Joe meets a member of AA who is able to help him to finally turn his life around. Kirstie isn't so lucky, and disappears from Joe's life. She returns one last time to say good-bye, and Joe must accept the fact that she is forever lost to him.

JOE CLAY

Shortly after the birth of their daughter, Joe comes home after a dinner party. He is drunk and becomes enraged when Kirstie refuses to drink with him because she is nursing the baby.

Well now, look: come home after a couple of drinks, and you're cold sober. Well, maybe you're a little tired or something. I know I seem loud and all right, I am! You didn't used to think so. I feel your disapproval. I feel it. Well, if you want to sit up—if you want to wait for me . . . well, is there any law that says you can't have a couple of blasts while you're waiting? Huh? Is there? So that maybe we could have some laughs around here? Is there? Yeah, your milk. Well, what is that bit anyhow? This is the twentieth century! They invented milk bottles and they got milk in cans that's as good as that milk! You're going to ruin your shape. For crying out loud, you'd think you were the only woman that ever had a baby. I was dragged around by the scruff of my neck on midnight trains and in freezing weather. I was eating crackers and . . . don't do that! I was eating peanut butter! Now, kids have got to learn to be people. Don't . . . look, please just get her a bottle and some formula because I want to have a ball, just you and me, see? Don't shush me! And if I'm too loud I'll just close the damn door!

KIRSTIE CLAY

Kirstie returns to Joe one last time and begs him to take her back. She seeks his forgiveness for the countless men she has been with and tearfully admits that she can never stop drinking completely.

Joe, I haven't had a drink in two days. It wasn't easy, but I wanted to talk to you so I thought I'd try and deserve it a little . . . sort of a penance you might say. Joe, wouldn't it be wonderful if we could go back to the beginning? Just erase everything in between—start all over? And getting excited over a chocolate bar. I want to come home. I know what you're thinking about. A lot's happened—lots of detours. There were plenty of them, but they were nothing. I never looked at them. They had no identity. I never gave anything out of myself to them. I thought they'd help me from being so lonely, but I was just as lonely because love is the only thing that keeps you from being lonely and I didn't have that. I don't know if I have the right words. That's why it took me so long to get here. You see, the world looks so dirty to me when I'm not drinking. Joe, remember Fisherman's Wharf? The water when you look too close? That's the way the world looks to me when I'm not drinking. I don't think I could ever stop drinking completely—not like you. If I wanted to— really wanted to? Well, I don't. I know that now. I want things to look prettier than they are. But I know I could be all right if you help me. I know I could be all right if we were together and things were like they used to be and I wasn't so nervous. I need to be loved. I get so lonely from not being loved, I can't stand it.

THE MANCHURIAN CANDIDATE

1962

MGM

Screenplay by George Axelrod
Based on a novel by Richard Condon
Directed by John Frankenheimer
Produced by George Axelrod and John Frankenheimer

1 MONOLOGUE
Mrs. Iselin

SETTING: Korea and the United States, 1952

This controversial thriller tells the story of Raymond Shaw, an army officer captured and brainwashed by the Communists during the Korean War. It is his captors' intention to transform him into a killer so that he will do their bidding at a moment's notice. Shaw and his men are released, and all memories prior to their brainwashing are erased from their minds.

Major Bennet Marco was captured along with Shaw. Soon after his return to the United States, he begins to have nightmares that tell the awful story of their time at the Communist indoctrination center. Marco is finally able to unravel the mystery, and realizes that Shaw is now an unwitting tool of the enemy.

Shaw's mother is married to Senator Iselin, a hard-line conservative who is vying for the presidential nomination. Mrs. Iselin is a ruthless woman who is capable of anything—even selling out to the Communists—to satisfy her lust for power. She has been in league with the enemy from the beginning, using her foolish husband to achieve a position of prominence and influence. She reveals all to her son on the eve of the convention, for he has been trained to assassinate the party nominee. Although she grieves for the loss of her son's mind, she revels in the victory she believes to be close at hand.

Marco races to the convention center in a desperate attempt to stop the assassination. As he searches the huge complex for a sign of Shaw, the assassin sets his sights on the presidential nominee. Marco finally breaks into the room where Shaw is hiding, but it is too late. Shaw fires, but at his mother; killing her. He then turns the gun on himself, ending his nightmare forever.

MRS. ISELIN

Mrs. Iselin reveals her part in the Manchurian conspiracy to her son. She mourns the loss of his mind and personhood and dreams of the glory of the revolution to come.

It's been decided that you will be dressed as a priest—to help you get away in the pandemonium. Afterwards, Chun Chin will give you a two-piece Soviet sniper rifle that fits nicely into a special bag. There's a spotlight booth that won't be in use. It's up under the roof on the Eighth Avenue side of the Garden. You will have absolutely clear, protected shooting. You are to shoot the presidential nominee through the head, and Johnny will rise gallantly to his feet and lift Ben Arthur's body in his arms and stand in front of the microphones and begin to speak. The speech is short, but it's the most rousing speech I've ever read. It's been worked on here and in Russia on and off for over eight years. I shall force someone to take the body away from him and Johnny will really hit those microphones and those cameras with blood all over him—fighting off anyone who tries to help him—defending America even if it means his own death; rallying a nation of television viewers into hysteria to sweep us up into the White House with powers that will make martial law seem like anarchy. Now, this is very important: I want the nominee to be dead about two minutes after he begins his acceptance speech—depending upon his reading time under pressure. You are to hit him right at the point when he finishes the phrase, ". . . nor would I ask of any fellow American in defense of his freedom that which I would not gladly give myself. My life before my liberty." Is that absolutely clear? I know you will never entirely comprehend this, Raymond, but you must believe I did not know it would be you. I served them. I fought for them. I'm on the point of winning for them the greatest foothold they will ever have in this country, and they paid me back by taking your soul away from you. I told them to build me an assassin. I wanted a killer from a world filled with killers and they chose you because they thought it would bind me closer to them. But now we have come almost to the end—one last step, and then when I take power they will be pulled down and ground into dirt for what they did to you—and what they did in so contemptuously underestimating me.

THE HAUNTING

1963

MGM
Screenplay by Nelson Gidding
Based on the novel The Haunting of Hill House
by Shirley Jackson
Directed and Produced by Robert Wise

3 MONOLOGUES
Eleanor 1
Eleanor 2
Eleanor 3

SETTING: New England, early 1960s

Hill House is a huge mansion in the backwoods of New England with an unsavory past. Some claim the house was "born bad" and others claim the disturbances are the result of earth tremors and sunspots. Whatever the source of the trouble, the end result is clear: insanity and death for all who enter.

Dr. John Marquey, a noted parapsychologist, leases Hill House with the intent of conducting a scientific study of the paranormal within its walls. He invites Theodora, a famous medium, and Eleanor Lance, a lonely woman who was the victim of a poltergeist attack when she was a child, to help him conduct his experiments. Eleanor has taken care of her invalid mother all her life and, with her mother's death, is finally free to do as she likes.

Sensitive Eleanor immediately falls under the evil spell of Hill House. As the days go by she seems to be disappearing little by little into the house as her faltering sense of identity slips away. John urges Eleanor to leave, but his concern is too late. As she drives away from the house an alien force takes control of her car and crashes it into a tree in the exact spot where the first lady of the house was killed in a carriage accident. Hill House has claimed another victim.

ELEANOR 1

Eleanor has been living with her sister and brother-in-law since the death of her mother. She feels a prisoner in their home and rejoices at the opportunity to strike out on her own.

(*Reading from a letter from John.*) "Very happy that you'll be joining us at Hill House. Take US 50 from Boston and watch for the turn-off onto Route 238." Route 238. At last I'm going someplace where I am expected and where I am being given shelter and I shall never have to come back. I hope . . . I hope . . . I hope this is what I have been waiting for all my life. I'm going. I'm really going. I've finally taken a step. By now they know the car is gone. But they don't know where. They would never have suspected it of me. I would never have suspected it of myself. I'm a new person. Someday . . . someday . . . someday I'll have an apartment of my own—in a house with a pair of stone lions guarding the gate. I might just stop anywhere and never leave again. Or I might drive on and on, until the wheels of the car are worn to nothing and I've come to the end of the world. I wonder if all homeless people feel that way?

ELEANOR 2

After several days in Hill House, Eleanor begins to fear for her sanity. Here, she tells John about the death of her mother.

Maybe I am insane. My mother . . . The night my mother died, she knocked on the wall and I didn't come. Eleven years of looking in on her after every small noise, but that night my back hurt . . . and my hands . . . It wasn't fair, we could have afforded a laundress. I ought to have brought her medicine. I always did before, but this time she called me and I never answered. Is that how a normal person acts? My sister says I wanted mother to die. I've wondered ever since if I didn't wake up in the night and hear her . . . just go back to sleep . . . it would have been easy. I've wondered about it.

ELEANOR 3

John's skeptical wife arrives at Hill House to persuade her husband to give up his work. In the night, she disappears from her bedroom during a full-fledged paranormal attack. In the confusion, Eleanor wanders the halls of Hill House and realizes that she has finally come home.

I'm coming apart a little at a time . . . a little at a time. Now I know where I'm going: I'm disappearing inch by inch into this house. I want to stay here. I want to stay here always. I will not be frightened or alone anymore. Here I am. Here I am inside and it's not cold at all. And the smell is gone. I've broken the spell of Hill House. I'm home . . . I'm home . . . I'm home . . . I'm home. No stone lions for me. I am home.

OF HUMAN BONDAGE

1964

MGM
A Seven Arts Production
Screenplay by Bryan Forbes
Additional Scenes by Henry Hathaway
Based on the novel by W. Somerset Maugham
Directed by Kenneth Hughes
Produced by James Woolf

1 MONOLOGUE
Mildred Rogers

SETTING: Victorian England

Of Human Bondage is W. Somerset Maugham's dark tale of one man's desperate love for a woman of low morals and of her inability to reciprocate his devotion. Philip Carey is a young medical student who first meets Mildred Rogers at the university pub where she is a waitress. He is captivated by her beauty and is soon infatuated.

Despite the handicap of a club foot, Philip pursues Mildred relentlessly, ignoring warnings from friends who are quick to point to her less than wholesome reputation. Mildred at first seems delighted by Philip's ardor, but she is ultimately incapable of returning his love. A woman of great pride and passion, Mildred values her freedom more than a future as Philip's wife.

Mildred continues to drift in and out of Philip's life, nearly destroying him both financially and emotionally. He takes her in when she is destitute and pregnant, but she leaves him yet again. He finally realizes that he must push her out of his heart. Over the years that follow, he hears rumors that Mildred is walking the streets. The rumors are substantiated when Mildred finally appears in Philip's clinic—ravaged by syphilis. Mildred dies in Philip's arms, and at last he is free to live his own life.

MILDRED ROGERS

In an emotional confrontation, Mildred reveals her true nature to Philip. She has used his blind love to further her own ends, and she relishes making him feel the fool.

I disgust you? Oh, that's a laugh—I disgust *you?* You're the one to talk, I suppose. I suppose you think you're God's gift to women or something. Well, you're nothing! That's all you're fit for, all you can do is think about it—like some dirty little school boy. It's all up here with you. Do you know what I think about you? You ought to take a look at yourself. I used to laugh at you. I still laugh at you. Because you were too easy—you bored me. I hated you for being so easy. I could just twist you any way I wanted to. I'd feel sick when I let you kiss me. Do you know that? I felt sick. I felt sick. Afterwards, after I let you, do you know what I did? I used to wipe my mouth. Well, I got my own back. We laughed at you—Miller and me, and Griffiths and me especially. Yes, Griffiths laughed at you. We used to talk about you when I was in bed with them—when they were making love to me. Know what we used to call you? I used to say, "Wouldn't the cripple like to be here kissing me now?" Because that's all you are—just a cripple! A bloody cripple!

THE AGONY AND THE ECSTASY

1965

20th Century-Fox
Screenplay by Philip Dunne
Based on the novel by Irving Stone
Directed and Produced by Carol Reed

1 MONOLOGUE
Michelangelo

SETTING: 16th-Century Rome

The Agony and the Ecstasy tells the story of Michelangelo's volatile relationship with his patron, Pope Julius II, and of the painting of the ceiling of the Sistine Chapel.

At Julius' insistence, Michelangelo was forced to abandon his first love, sculpture, to "decorate" the chapel. Driven by passion, the man who considered painting not to be his medium created the magnificent frescoes which depict the creation of man by God. As war raged around Rome, pope and artist waged their own private war of wills, but as the pope learned that genius is something that cannot be forced or contained, Michelangelo learned to tap his love for life and translate it into the frescoes.

The film ends with the ceiling's completion. The two very different men who have worked so hard for so long to create one of the world's greatest testimonies to man's love for God must now separate and follow their individual destinies.

MICHELANGELO

When confronted by an old love, Michelangelo explains that he can no longer love people. He is too consumed by passion for his work.

In Florence, years ago, I loved you. I loved you. But now, there's no room in me for love. Maybe there never was. I wondered about that. In Bologna, there was a woman, a courtesan—beautiful. I was attracted to her, made love to her, even wrote a sonnet to her. It was a poor thing—the words meant nothing because she meant nothing. Less than nothing. It left me empty. After that I prayed—prayed for understanding. Maybe God crippled me—with a purpose as He does often. The bird is weak—He gives it wings. The deer is helpless—He made is swift. He made Homer blind, let him see the world more clearly than any other man. He gave me the power to create, to fashion my own kind, but only here, in these *(indicates hands)*. To other men he gives warm houses, women, children, laughter . . . to me . . .

ANNE OF THE THOUSAND DAYS

1969

Universal Studios
Screenplay by John Hale and Bridget Boland
Directed by Charles Jarrott
Produced by Hal B. Wallis

2 MONOLOGUES
Henry VIII
Anne Boleyn

SETTING: 16th-century England—the court of Henry VIII.

This is the tale of the tempestuous and ill-fated love affair of Henry VIII and Anne Boleyn: kindred souls filled with passion and lust for power.

Henry married his dead brother's wife to seal a political breach. He was soon frustrated by the loveless marriage, and his wandering eye then turned to the many ladies of his court. Henry's sexual exploits were the stuff that legend is made of, for no woman dared deny the king—no woman, with the exception of Anne Boleyn.

Attracted by her youth and innocence, Henry summons her to court only to be met with a flat refusal. Enraged, the vengeful Henry commands that she become a lady-in-waiting and thereby be forced to see him every day. Anne soon learns the intricacies of the delicate balance of power in Henry's court and delights in using her new-found power to torment the king.

Henry becomes increasingly besotted with Anne, and favors her with many privileges. Anne tells Henry that she will never sleep with him unless it is as his wife. Made desperate by his desire, Henry asks his wife, Catherine, for an anullment. When she refuses, the only option remaining is divorce.

Henry moves heaven and hell to accomplish this, cutting England off from Rome and antagonizing Spain in the process. When Anne and Henry are finally wed, she bears him a child; Elizabeth. Henry, wanting a son, begins to lose interest in Anne.

Another pregnancy which results in a stillbirth of a female child pushes him even further away. Since Anne is no longer any use to him, Henry begins to plot her demise. She is charged with treason, found guilty, and executed. A mere one thousand days after becoming queen. The rest, as they say, is history.

HENRY VIII

Henry confronts Anne after he has signed death warrants condemning those who oppose their marriage. The king is exhausted, and is beginning to question his desire.

That is the rest of them that would dare question. The rest will die— silent. I think there has never been a king who gave so much to find his way to the heart of the woman he loved. I've stabbed, and fought, and clawed my way through the tissues of the Church and the State. I've looted and plundered. I've ripped and torn the bodies of my friends. And all to come to this day. Yet not once, not once you said, "I love you." Now, my Nan, my Nan, will you say it now? No, that's not it. That's not what I meant. I don't know. I don't know, Nan, but I still don't have you. Tell me, Nan, did someone someday say to you, "Never give in to him. Never melt to him. Never forget to hate him for a time. Otherwise you will lose him?" Keep your heart, then. Preserve your special chastity. I'm too old to suffer the longings and passions and frenzy of a stupid boy—writing poems in the middle of the night to the cold-hearted bitch that I love and tearing them up. Pacing up and down, pacing up and down in my room unable to sleep. Sons you have promised me when you are queen, and sons I will have. Sons without love if I must. Enjoy your palace. I will not come near you again until the marriage day.

ANNE BOLEYN

The queen reflects upon the thousand days that she has spent with Henry on the night before her execution. She laments the fact that there was only one day out of the thousand when they were both in love.

For six years, this year, this and this and this; I did not love him. And then I did. Then I was his. I can count the days I was his in hundreds. The days we bedded, married, were happy, born Elizabeth, hated, lusted, born dead child—which condemned me—the death. All in all, one thousand days. Just one thousand. Strange. And of those thousand, one where we're both in love. Only one when our loves met and overlapped and were both mine and his. When I no longer hated him, he began to hate me. Except for that one day.

HAROLD AND MAUDE

1971

Universal Pictures
Screenplay by Colin Higgins
Directed by Hal Ashby
Produced by Colin Higgins and Charles B. Mulvehill

2 MONOLOGUES
Mrs. Chasen
Harold

SETTING: The American Southwest, early 1970s

Harold Chasen is a young man with an unusual hobby: staging fake suicides to get his mother's attention. Hardly a day goes by in the sumptuous Chasen mansion without a hanging, shooting, stabbing, or poisoning.

Harold's mother is a shallow woman who believes that she can solve her son's problems by either enlisting him in the army or marrying him off. When he isn't busy dodging dates arranged by his mother, Harold likes to attend funerals. It is at a funeral that he first meets Maude, a seventy-nine-year-old widow who is possessed of a lust for living that any sixteen-year-old would envy.

Maude befriends the somber young man, and is eventually able to draw him out of his dark fantasy world. She teaches Harold how to enjoy life by endowing him with a touch of exuberance that was heretofore lacking in his soul. Harold falls in love with the vivacious Maude, and they begin a relationship. Harold is unaware, however, that Maude plans to commit suicide on her eightieth birthday. He informs his mother that he plans to marry Maude and goes to celebrate her birthday. By the time Maude tells him of her plan, she has taken the pills; it is too late to save her life. The master of fake suicides finds himself helpless when faced with reality.

Grief-stricken, Harold drives his car over a cliff. After it crashes, we see that he managed to jump out before it went over. All he has left is a banjo given to him by Maude which he strums as he heads off into the sunset.

MRS. CHASEN

Harold's mother has decided to enlist Harold in a computer dating club. She calls him into her study and reads through the questions on the application form. Harold never says a word as she fills in the blanks for him.

I have here, Harold, the form sent out by the National Computer Dating Service. They screen out the fat and the ugly; so it is obviously a firm of high standards. "Here is the personality interview which you are to fill out and return." Are you ready, Harold? Here is the first question. "Are you uncomfortable meeting new people?" Well, I think that's a 'yes.' Don't you agree, Harold? "Should sex education be taught outside the home?" I would say no, wouldn't you, Harold? We'll give a 'D' there. Three—"Should women run for president of the United States?" Well, I don't see why not. Absolutely, yes. "Do you remember jokes and take pleasure in relating them to others?" You don't do that, do you, Harold? No, absolutely no. "Do you often get the feeling that perhaps life isn't worth living?" Hmmm? What do you think, Harold? 'A'? 'B'? I'll put down 'C'—"not sure." "Is the subject of sex being over-exploited by our mass media?" That would have to be 'yes,' wouldn't it? "Is it difficult for you to accept criticism?" No. We'll mark 'D.' "Do you sometimes have headaches or backaches after a difficult day?" Yes, I do indeed! "Do you go to sleep easily?" I would say so. "Do you believe in capital punishment for murder?" Oh, yes. I do indeed. "In your opinion, are social affairs usually a waste of time?" Heavens, no. "Can God influence our lives?" Oh, yes. Absolutely yes. "Does your personal religion or philosophy include a life after death?" Oh, yes indeed. That's absolutely. "Did you enjoy life when you were a child?" Oh, yes. You were a wonderful baby, Harold. "Do you think the sexual revolution has gone too far?" It certainly has. "Do you find the idea of wife-swapping distasteful?" I find the question distasteful. "Do you have ups and downs without obvious reason?" That's you, Harold.

HAROLD

Harold finally breaks down and confesses to Maude the reason why he stages fake suicides.

I haven't lived. I've died a few times. The first time was in boarding school in the chemistry lab. I was cleaning it up. So, I decided I'd do a little experimenting, you know? So, I get all this stuff out and begin mixing it up. It was very scientific. There was this massive explosion. It knocked me down, blew a huge hole in the floor. There were boards and bricks and flames leaping up. I figured, you know, time to leave. My career in school was over. So I went home. My mother was giving a party, so I went right up the back stairs, turned out the light, and I got this funny feeling. The doorbell rang and these two policemen came in, found my mother and told her that I was killed in the fire. She put one hand up to her forehead, and the other she reached out, groping for support; and with this long sigh she collapsed in their arms. I decided right then, I enjoyed being dead.

JAWS

1975

Universal City Studios
Screenplay by Peter Benchley and Carl Gottlieb
Based on the novel by Peter Benchley
Directed by Steven Spielberg
Produced by Richard D. Zanuck and David Brown

1 MONOLOGUE
Quint

SETTING: Amity Island, 1975

Amity Island is terrorized by a giant great white shark in this tale of seaside terror. Police Chief Brody, a man with a fear of water, fights corrupt politicians and greedy shopkeepers to close the beaches which have become the shark's favorite feeding spots. Joined by Hooper, a young marine biologist, and Quint, a salty old sea dog with a thing for sharks, Brody takes to the sea to hunt and destroy the finned killer. The three very different men learn to rely upon one another as the game changes and they become the hunted. The shark pursues them for several days before a final confrontation ends in the bloody death of Quint and the shark. The two old adversaries float to the bottom of the sea as Hooper and Brody swim ashore.

QUINT

Brody, Hooper, and Quint settle down in the galley of Quint's boat after their first day of shark hunting. They trade stories and song, and Quint offers the following tale of his experience on the USS Indianapolis, *the ship that delivered the bomb that destroyed Hiroshima.*

Japanese submarine slammed two torpedos into our side, Chief. We
was coming back from the island of Tarawa. We'd just delivered the
bomb; the Hiroshima bomb. Eleven hundred men went into the
water. The vessel went down in twelve minutes. Didn't see the first
shark for about a half an hour. Tiger. Thirteen footer. You know
how you know that when you're in the water, Chief? You tell by
looking from the dorsal to the tail. Well, we didn't know, but our
bomb mission had been so secret, no distress signal had been sent.
They didn't even list us overdue for a week. Very first light, Chief,
sharks come cruisin'. So we formed ourselves into tight groups. You
know it's kind of like squares in a battle, like you see on a calendar;
like the Battle of Waterloo. The idea was, shark'd come to the near-
est man and he'd start pounding, hollering, and screaming. Sometimes the shark would go away, but sometimes he wouldn't go away.
Sometimes that shark—he looks right into your eyes. You know the
thing about a shark, he's got lifeless eyes, black eyes; like a doll's
eyes. When he comes at you, he doesn't seem to be living until he
bites you and those black eyes roll over white and then you hear
that terrible high-pitched screaming. The ocean turns red. Despite
all the pounding and the hollering, they all come in—rip you to
pieces. Nobody that first dawn. Lost a hundred men. I don't know
how many sharks, maybe a thousand. Don't know how many men;
we averaged six an hour. On Thursday morning, Chief, I bumped
into a friend of mine; Herbie Robertson from Cleveland. Baseball
player, bo's'n's mate, I thought he was asleep. Reached over to wake
him up. He bobbed up and down in the water just like a kind of top
upended. Well, he'd been bitten in half below the waist. Noon the
fifth day, Mr. Hooper, a Lockheed Ventura saw us. He swung in low
and he saw us. A young pilot—a lot younger than Mr. Hooper. Anyway, he saw us and he come in low and three hours later a big fat
PBY comes down and starts to pick us up. You know, that was the
time I was most frightened; waiting for my turn. I'll never put on a
lifejacket again. So, eleven hundred men went into the water; three
hundred and sixteen men came out. The sharks took the rest. June
the 29th, 1945. Anyway, we delivered the bomb.

TAXI DRIVER

1976

Columbia
Screenplay by Paul Schrader
Directed by Martin Scorsese
Produced by Michael Phillips and Julia Phillips

1 MONOLOGUE
Travis Bickel

SETTING: New York City, 1970s

Travis prowls the streets of New York at night, observing prostitution, drugs, and other unwholesome activities from behind the wheel of his taxi cab. A man on the edge, Travis is obsessed with the disintegration of society and has become filled with rage and despair. Travis falls in love with Betsy, a beautiful young woman who spurns him.

Pushed as far as he can go, Travis transforms himself into a killing machine. After an aborted attempt to assassinate a presidential candidate from which he escapes undetected, Travis tries to convince Iris, a young prostitute, to give up her life on the streets and return to her parents in the Midwest. When Iris's pimp discovers Travis in her room, a struggle ensues that leaves many dead and the now insane Travis wounded. Hailed as a hero for killing the pimps and reuniting Iris with her parents, Travis returns to his taxi cab and the dark streets of New York City.

TRAVIS BICKEL

Travis relates his feelings about life on the streets in his journal.

All the animals come out at night. Whores, skunk pussies, buggers, queens, fairies, dopers, junkies. Sick; venal. Someday, a real rain will come and wash all this scum off the streets. I go all over. I take people to the Bronx, Brooklyn—I take them to Harlem. I don't care. Don't make no difference to me. It does to some. Some won't even take the spooks. Don't make no difference to me. Twelve hours of work and I still can't sleep. Damn. The days go on and on. They don't end. All my life needed was a sense of someplace to go. I don't believe that one should devote his time to morbid self-attention. I believe that someone should become a person like other people.

COMING HOME

1978

United Artists
Screenplay by Waldo Scott and Robert C. Jones
Story by Nancy Dowd
Directed by Hal Ashby
Produced by Jerome Hellman

1 MONOLOGUE
Luke Martin

SETTING: California, 1960s

When Sally Hyde's husband is sent to Vietnam, she decides to do volunteer work at the local VA hospital. There she encounters Luke Martin, her teenage heartthrob, whose experience in Vietnam has left him a quadriplegic. Despite Luke's bitterness, he and Sally become friends. In a quickly changing society, Sally is often bewildered by the many conflicting views of the war and finds herself torn between her love for her Marine husband and her growing feelings for Luke.

Bob Hyde returns from Vietnam a shattered man. His bravado and blind patriotism have been destroyed by the horrific reality of war. Discovering that Sally has slept with Luke pushes him over the edge, and he is driven to take his own life.

LUKE

Luke reveals his feeling for Sally in this monologue which also reveals his acceptance of his quadriplegia.

Do you know that when I dream, I'm not in the chair. I don't even have a chair. In my dream I have legs. When I was a kid I used to jump in my mother's kitchen and touch the ceiling. She used to get pissed-off because I'd leave my hand prints in the ceiling. You know, I still check the snow reports—the conditions at Mamouth. I'm still the same person. It's funny: people look at me, they see something else, but they don't see who I am, you know? You know, I spend about ninety-five percent of my time at the hospital thinking about making love with you.

... AND JUSTICE FOR ALL

1979

Columbia Pictures
Screenplay by Valerie Curtin and Barry Levinson
Directed by Norman Jewison
Produced by Norman Jewison and Patrick Palmer

1 MONOLOGUE
Arthur Kirkland

SETTING: The United States, 1970s

As an ethical lawyer, Arthur Kirkland represents an endangered species in this black comedy of the American justice system. Arthur must battle corrupt judges, crazy partners, and an investigation by the Ethics Committee on his journey through the quagmire of legal bureaucracy that surrounds his profession.

One of Arthur's clients, McCollough, has been wrongly imprisoned, and although Arthur tries desperately to gain his release, all pleas to the Honorable Henry T. Fleming go unanswered.

The very same judge is arrested and charged with rape and, in an ironic twist, he hires Arthur to handle his defense. Before Arthur can strike a deal with Fleming to release his client, McCollough is killed in an attempted escape. By this time Arthur has received photographic evidence that proves Fleming's guilt. Shocked by McCollough's death and Fleming's guilt in the rape case, Arthur arrives in court and gives the most sensational speech of his career.

Arthur is removed from the courtroom and as the film ends, he is thrust back into the real world of the streets, his career and idealism shattered.

ARTHUR KIRKLAND

In this emotional outburst, Kirkland reveals to the packed courtroom that his client is guilty and that the legal system is a sham.

Your Honor, Mr. Foreman, ladies and gentlemen of the jury. My name is Arthur Kirkland and I am the defense counsel for the defendant, Henry T. Fleming. Now, I'm saying Henry T. Fleming, because if I say *Judge* Henry T. Fleming, then I get angry. And a little embarrassed. Aren't you a little embarrassed? I mean, he's a judge. Now *that* man . . . the prosecuting attorney . . . he couldn't be happier. He's a happy man today. He's going after a judge. And if he gets him, he's going to be a star. He's going to be the centerfold in this year's Law Review. Now, to win this case he needs your help, because you're all he has. He's counting on tapping that emotion that says "Let's get somebody in power." Because, let's face it, we're all skeptical of those in power. We've all been burned. But what is the purpose of these proceedings? To see that justice prevails. And I'm sure that every reasonable person would agree that justice is the finding of truth. Now one truth, a tragic one, is that a young girl has been brutally raped. Another truth is that the prosecution does not have one witness, not one substantiating piece of evidence other than the testimony of the victim herself. And another truth is that the prosecution is well aware that Henry T. Fleming voluntarily took a lie detector test and passed it! He told the truth!!! That's inadmissible evidence and pretend I didn't say it. Disregard that remark. I'm sorry Your Honor. What is the intention of justice? To see that the guilty go to jail and the innocent go free. But it isn't as simple as that. Did you know that ninety percent of the people a defense attorney represents are guilty? Did you know that? Interesting, isn't it? Ninety percent. So that means when we fight to win a case, we are fighting to put a lot of guilty people back out on the streets as soon as possible. Where is the justice in that? Well, you see, it is the duty of the defense lawyer to uphold the rights of the individual . . . and it's the prosecution's job to see that the laws of society are upheld. JUSTICE FOR ALL! But we have a problem, don't we? Both sides want to win. Regardless of guilt or innocence. Regardless of the truth, then regardless of justice. Winning becomes all. I won that case—You know, I won three cases in a row, then I won six more. I didn't even think I was going to win that one—but I won. It becomes a game—a game. And I intend to win this one. The prosecution is not going to get this man . . . because I'm going to get him. My client, the Honorable Henry T. Fleming, should go right to fuckin' jail. The son-of-a-bitch is guilty! If this man is allowed to go free, something very wrong is going on here! The man is slime! He is slime! The trial is a show! That man, that depraved, crazy man raped this girl here. And he'd like to do it again! He told me that! It's all coming apart! It's just a show. It's "Let's Make A Deal"! You want to make a deal? C'mon, Frank. I've got one insane judge who likes to beat the shit out of girls. What do you want to give me? Three weeks probation? You're supposed to stand for something, you son-of-a-bitch! You're supposed to protect people and instead you fuck and murder them! Hold it! Hold it! Okay! Okay! . . . I have completed my opening statement!

BLADE RUNNER

1982

Warner Brothers
Screenplay by Hampton Francher and David Peoples
Based on the novel Do Androids Dream of Electric Sheep?
by Phillip K. Dick
Directed by Ridley Scott
Produced by Michael Deeley

1 MONOLOGUE
Roy Blatty

SETTING: Los Angeles, 2019

A Blade Runner is a member of an elite police squad whose job it is to "retire" replicants (androids) who have broken the law. The story centers around Dekert, an ex–Blade Runner who is called back into service against his will to hunt down and destroy four renegade replicants who have returned to earth to seek out their creator. Replicants are so nearly human that only hours of testing can determine the difference.

Dekert feels that he has become an executioner and grapples with many moral issues as he finds himself falling in love with Rachel, a beautiful woman who doesn't know that she is, in fact, a replicant.

Dekert pursues the runaway replicants; Roy, Leon, Zora, and Pris, destroying them one by one until only the formidable Roy is left. In the dramatic climax of the film, a wounded Dekert is pursued by a wrathful Roy through a ruined L.A. skyscraper. Replicants are only given a four year life span, and Roy's time is nearly up. He rages at Dekert as he chases him to the rooftop, seeing in Dekert's humanity all the things he's ever wanted but will never have. Then, in an unforgettable moment, Roy saves Dekert's life; proving that in many ways, replicants have their own humanity. The two exhausted men collapse on the rooftop, and Dekert watches as Roy "dies."

ROY BLATTY

This monologue begins with Roy's pursuit of Dekert through the crumbling skyscraper and ends with his death. As he pursues a frightened Dekert, the angry replicant expresses a range of very human emotions.

Not very sporting to fire on an unarmed opponent. I thought you were supposed to be good. Aren't you the good man? Come out, Dekert! Show me what you're made of. Proud of yourself, little man? Come on Dekert! I'm right here. But you've got to shoot straight. Straight doesn't seem to be good enough. Now it's my turn. I'm going to give you a few seconds before I come. One, two, three, four. I'm coming, Dekert! Four, five; how to stay alive. I can see you! Not yet, not yet! You better get it up, or I'm going to have to kill you. Unless you're alive, you can't play, and if you can't play . . . six, seven; go to hell or go to heaven. That's the spirit! That hurt. That was irrational of you. Not to mention unsportsmanlike. Where are you going? Quite an experience to live in fear, isn't it? That's what it is; to be a slave. I've seen things you people wouldn't believe. Attack ships on fire off the shoulder of Orion. I watched seabeams glitter in the dark near the Tannhauser Gate. All those moments will be lost in time, like tears in rain. Time to die.

KING OF COMEDY

1982

Embassy International
Screenplay by Paul D. Zimmerman
Directed by Martin Scorsese
Produced by Arnon Milchan

1 MONOLOGUE
Marsha

SETTING: New York City, 1982

Rupert Pupkin wants to be a stand-up comedian. More specifically, he wants to be the King of Comedy. It is his dream to appear on the Jerry Langford show, a Johnny Carson–style talk show whose host he idolizes. Rupert waits outside the studio every day, hoping for an opportunity to speak with his hero, Jerry. Joining him in this endeavor is Marsha, a psychotic young woman who is also obsessed with Jerry.

Driven over the edge by Jerry's rejection of a tape of his comedy monologue, Rupert joins with Marsha in a plot to kidnap Jerry. When they have the talk-show host in their clutches, Rupert notifies the show's producer that unless he is allowed to present his comedy monologue on the show, they will never see Jerry alive again.

Rupert is arrested immediately after the show, but spends his time in jail writing a best-seller that will forever confirm his place as the King of Comedy.

MARSHA

Crazy Marsha lives out many fantasies as she tells a bound and gagged Jerry about her feelings for him. Toward the end of her monologue, she loses control and practically rapes Jerry.

I feel completely impulsive tonight. Anything—anything could happen. I've so much to tell you. I don't know where to start. I just want to tell you everything. I want to tell you everything about myself. Everything you don't know. Do you like these glasses? Crystal; beautiful. I bought them just for you. I don't know, something about them reminded me—just the simplicity of them—but if you don't like them, if there's even an inkling that you have doubt in your mind . . . You know, sometimes during the day I'll just be doing the simplest things, you know, I'll be taking a bath, and I'll say to myself, "I wonder if Jerry's taking a bath right now?" And I just hope you're not drowning or something. I just get really worried about you, you know, like something terrible is going to happen. And then I'll have, like, these day dreams, like you know, like I'm out with you at the golf course, driving in a cart—just driving around. "Need a putter, Jer?" You know. "Need an iron?" I don't know how to play golf. I played with my parents once. My dad. I love you. I've never told my parents that I love them. Of course, they've never told me that they love me, either; which is fine with me. But, I love you. Want some wine? No? Okay. I'm not in the mood to drink either. But I'm sure in the mood to be alone with you. Why don't we just clear off the table? I was thinking that we ought to go upstairs, but that's so predictable. Let's just take everything off the table and do it right here. Betcha that would blow your mind, wouldn't it? It would blow my mind. I've never done anything like that before. I've never had anybody over for dinner, let alone made love on the table. But somehow, I just want to do that. I just want to, like, dance. I just want to, like—you know, put on some Shirelles. I want to be black. Wouldn't that be insane? God, I wish I was— you know who I wish I was tonight? I wish I was Tina Turner, just dancing through the room. Let's do something crazy tonight. Just get insane. I want to be crazy. I want to be nuts. I want some fun, god damn it. My doctor says, "Don't have any fun. You can't have fun. No, you're not allowed to have a good time. You can't get crazy." See, I have to be in control, and I like being in control, but you know—for one night I'd like to see myself out of my head. Wouldn't you like to see me out of my head? Wouldn't it be great? Wouldn't it be fabulous? I'm having a good time. I'm having fun. Fun is my middle name. That's right, having some fun. I've never had this much fun before. That's right, good old fashioned all-American fun.

NATE AND HAYES

1983

Paramount Pictures
Screenplay by John Hughes
Directed by Ferdinand Fairfax
Produced by Lloyd Phillips and Rob Whitehouse

1 MONOLOGUE
"Bully" Hayes

SETTING: The islands of the South Pacific, mid-1800s

Nate and Hayes is the swashbuckling saga of "Bully" Hayes, a self-proclaimed pirate whose involvement with a young American missionary couple lands him on the gallows.

Bully is hired to sail the Reverend Nathaniel and his beautiful bride Sophie to the island where the Reverend's uncle has a mission. During the long voyage, Sophie becomes infatuated with the rugged Bully, much to the ire of the straight-laced Reverend Nathaniel.

Bully deposits the young couple on the island and then sails off into the sunset, leaving a smitten Sophie to stare after his ship, *The Rona*. In the middle of Nathaniel and Sophie's wedding ceremony, the beautiful island is attacked by blackbirders—slavers—led by the vicious Ben Pease. Nathaniel is struck down and left for dead while Sophie is taken by Pease—who just happens to be Bully's worst enemy.

Nathaniel must join forces with Bully to reclaim his Sophie and the two men soon become friends. Their search leads them to Samoa, where Bully learns that Pease is taking Sophie to Panape, a dangerous island desired by the German navy for deep anchorage. After battling cannibals and a German steam ship at Panape, they rescue Sophie. To her surprise, Nathaniel—or Nate, as he is now called by Bully and his buccaneers—is no longer the prim minister that she thought had died during the blackbird raid. She has found her true love at last.

"BULLY" HAYES

As the film opens, Bully has been arrested by the Spanish government for selling guns to the natives. As he awaits the gallows, he tells a journalist his life story in the dank cell that is to be his final home.

Are you writing down in that book that I'm a pirate? Good. 'Cause I am, and a damn good one, too. No, I never flew the skull and crossbones. That's for your fictioneers. But I have sought pleasure and profit all my life at sea with no regard for anyone's law. That's not to say without morals and standards. I got morals and standards. I never killed anybody who didn't have it coming. I've never cheated an honest man. I've never pillaged and I've never raped. It's hard to love a ship. They rot. But memories; Lord God I've got memories. I can't regret dying today. Hell, I've lived more than any man deserves. Bully. Call me Bully. The *Rona*, I suppose, is what put my neck in the noose today. Yes, she was a damn good ship. Nothing to be proud of, you understand, but she did her job without complaint. We'd been two months hauling this young couple across the Pacific Ocean in time for their wedding on some mission island. He planned to live there and convert the heathens; which to me seemed like a great waste of her. She was the finest thing I ever saw.

REPO MAN

1983

Universal Studios
Screenplay by Alex Cox
Directed by Alex Cox
Produced by Jonathan Wacks and Peter McCarthy

2 MONOLOGUES
Repo Man
Miller

SETTING: Los Angeles, 1980s

Repo Man is the story of Otto, an alienated youth whose nihilistic personality prevents him from finding a "normal" job.

Otto is eventually taken under the wing of a crafty repo man who teaches the young punk everything he needs to know about repossessing cars. Meanwhile, an alien spacecraft has crash-landed in the desert. A member of a secret UFO organization has absconded with the alien corpses and is driving them to LA in the trunk of his car. The radiation and whatever other cosmic forces are evident in the dead extraterrestrials gradually encompasses the car and driver—turning both into a potentially lethal weapon.

The car turns up on the repo computer printout, and all repo men are on the lookout for it. This modern fantasy comes to a close when Miller, the brain-fried handyman who works for the repo company, drives the car up over the city and out of sight.

REPO MAN

The experienced repo man gives young Otto a lecture on the "Repo Code" while they stop at a convenience store for some drinks. The store is held up by friends of Otto while they stand at the counter, but Repo Man never breaks stride.

I never broke into a car. I never hot-wired a car, kid. I never broke into a truck. I shall not cause harm to any vehicle nor the personal contents thereof; nor, through inaction, let that vehicle or the personal contents thereof come to harm. That's what I call the "Repo Code," kid. Don't forget it. Etch it in your brain. Not many people got a code to live by anymore. Hey, look at that! Look at those assholes over there. Ordinary fucking people. I hate 'em. What do you know, kid? See, an ordinary person spends his life avoiding tense situations. Repo Man spends his life getting into tense situations. Assholes. Let's go get a drink. Tense situations, kid. Get into five, six of them a day and it don't mean shit anymore. I mean, I've seen men stabbed and it didn't mean shit. I mean, I've seen guns, too. They don't mean shit. But that's when you gotta watch yourself. Here, I'll handle it, pal. Try to settle down. Have a nice day—right. Night, day—it doesn't mean shit. There's gonna be some bad shit coming down one of these days, kid. I'm gonna be right here, heading north at one-ten per.

MILLER

The weirdly esoteric handyman explains his theory of coincidence to a confused Otto. As his theory gets more and more complex, Otto begins to suspect that he took too much acid back in the '60s.

A lot of people don't realize what's really going on. They view life as a bunch of unconnected incidents and things. They don't realize that there's this, like, lattice of coincidence that lays on top of everything. I'll give you an example, show you what I mean: Suppose you're thinking about a plate of shrimp. Suddenly somebody will say, like, plate or shrimp or plate of shrimp out of the blue—no explanations. No point in looking for one either. It's all part of a cosmic unconsciousness. I'll give you another instance. You know the way everybody's into weirdness right now? Books in all the supermarkets about Bermuda Triangles, UFOs, how the Mayans invented television—that kind of thing? Well, the way I see it, it's exactly the same. There ain't no difference between a flying saucer and a time machine. People get so hung up on specifics they miss out on seeing the whole thing. Take South America for example. In South America, thousands of people go missing every year. Nobody knows where they go. They just, like, disappear. But if you think about it for a minute, you realize something. There had to be a time when there was no people, right? Well, where did all these people come from? Hmm? I'll tell you where: the future. Where did all these people disappear to? And how did they get there? Flying saucers! Which are really—yeah, you got it: time machines! I think a lot about this kind of stuff. I do my best thinking on the bus. That's how come I don't drive, see? I don't want to know how. I don't ever want to learn, see? The more you drive, the less intelligent you are.

REUBEN, REUBEN

1983

20th Century-Fox
Screenplay by Julius J. Epstein
Based on the novel by Peter de Vries
and the play "Spofford" by Herman Shumlin
Directed by Robert Ellis Miller
Produced by Walter Shenson

2 MONOLOGUES
Gowan McGland 1
Gowan McGland 2

SETTING: A small town in New England, 1980s

Reuben, Reuben is the story of Gowan McGland, a world-renowned poet whose alcoholic debauchery has prevented him from writing poetry for years. To support himself, Gowan travels the small-town lecture circuit where he encounters amorous wealthy housewives who are only too happy to subsidize his life-style in return for temporary attention and affection.

Gowan's ex-wife Edith has been offered a small fortune to write a biography of McGland, and has traveled to New York to discuss the project with him. On the train back to the small New England town where he has been speaking, he encounters beautiful young Geneva, with whom he falls in love. Geneva is a bright young college student who is quite taken with the poet's attentions. She soon falls under his spell, and despite her family's disapproval, becomes Gowan's lover.

Their love affair is doomed, for Gowan's alcoholism has progressed beyond the point where he can maintain a functional relationship. When a pregnant Geneva breaks it off with him, he falls into despair and plans to hang himself. As he ties the noose and sets

up the chair, he addresses his ex-wife Edith on the small tape recorder she has given him. Atop the chair with the noose around his
neck, Gowan speaks of his loss and suddenly creates a new poem.
So enraptured is he by this long-awaited breakthrough that he decides to go on living. Unfortunately, just at that moment, Reuben—
the old English Sheepdog belonging to Geneva's grandfather—bounds
into his room and knocks the chair out from under him.

GOWAN McGLAND 1

*The poet talks to Edith on the tape recorder she has given him in hopes that he
will provide material for her book on his life. He tells her of his love for Geneva.*

Edith, my dear one—here's a chapter for your filthy book. I'm in
love, Edith. Picture this, if you will: they're standing at the portal
to her modest home; to my horror, I hear myself saying to this young
girl, "May I walk you home from church?" Can you believe it? Just
to be in the same spirit-chilling edifice; to breathe the same stale air
as this strapping girl with rousing breasts and hair like ripe wheat.
Hips that sway like a bell and large eyes the color of cornflowers.
She's a radiant creature, Edith. Glowing with that light that seems
to come from within healthy young girls. God, my heart bleeds for
the raw youths that she must entrance and torment. There is after
all, Edith, no aphrodisiac like innocence.

GOWAN McGLAND 2

*As he prepares to kill himself, Gowan speaks one last time to Edith on
the tape recorder. As he addresses his grief over losing Geneva and his
despair of being told that he will lose his teeth, his years of writer's block
dissolve as he begins to compose a poem.*

And she walked off, and like a well-cast heroine she did not look back.
When she said, "Do you think it would be best if we didn't see each

other again?" I said yes, I think it would be for the best. My voice rang like a handful of false coins. And so, dear Edith, I have a gift for you: the ending of your book. I will record for you the last stray thoughts— the final sensations of your protagonist, Gowan Evans McGland. As I left Dr. Ormsby's office, as I descended the stairs as in a dream, I knew the destination to which I was moving. I'd always known for me, tooth- lessness—toothlessness would be the moment of truth. Toothlessness is for me chief in the range of cosmic insults heaped upon man—proof of his being totally and tragically ludicrous. A sign that for me, living was no longer endurable. In the long stategic retreat of life I've always seen myself as backing towards my grave. Tooth by tooth and poem by poem. I'll go to my grave voluntarily, Christ! Voluntarily, Edith! With a few of each still left in my head. Christ. I keep thinking of Geneva. As we sat in the town square, I experienced one last vast plummet of yearn- ing—to reach her and hold her. And resisting that was probably the single act of self-mastery I have ever performed. Well, that's more rea- son for my departure now, not less. Even if she chose to have the baby. I can give my child a heritage as long as I'm not around to spoil it. You know, Edith, my very last thought: it's funny, my regret is the poem I never finished. Do you remember that one that we both liked so much? "Come, let us spread a picnic on the precipice. Eat, drink, and be merry with our backs to the abyss 'til dusk when bats cannot be told from swallows. Gifts from threats will banish solemn songs like this . . ." Banish solemn songs like this. I could never finish that one, could I? God damn it! Could never finish it. Hopeless. This is our hopeless heaven. This is our hopeless heaven. These flowers our eyes have wa- tered. That's quite good! That's quite good, Edith. These flowers our eyes have watered. Wine drawn from our veins. Tunes piped from hol- lowed bones and gaiety pouring from every wound—Edith, gaiety pour- ing from every wound is good, isn't it? Edith, you better type it out and send it to somebody—you're so bloody helpless, I'll do it myself. Edith, does this mean, then, that I'm really too chicken to go through with this? I think it does, Edith. Well, why should I—why the hell should I? God damn it to bloody hell! There are still poems to be written, Edith! There are still women to be made love to. Including you, including you, my dearest Edith.

SOMETHING WICKED
THIS WAY COMES

1983

Walt Disney Productions
Screenplay by Ray Bradbury
Based on his novel
Directed by Jack Clayton
Produced by Peter Vincent Douglas

2 MONOLOGUES
Will Halloway
Mr. Halloway

SETTING: Rural Illinois, 1930s

This story of a father's love for his son begins on a perfect autumn day in mythic Greentown, Illinois. Young Will Halloway and Jim Nightshade are best friends. Together they know every inch of Greentown. Will's father is the town librarian, a quiet man who is somewhat old to have such a young son. Jim's father disappeared several years before, leaving his son to fantasize that his father is a daring adventurer who will someday return.

The two boys sneak out of their beds one night, and discover that a mysterious carnival has come to town. They creep up to the fairgrounds and watch, horrified, as the rides and attractions are set up. The sign reads: "Dark's Pandemonium Carnival."

The next day, everyone from Greentown goes to the carnival and strange things begin to happen. Mr. Crosetti, the town barber who always dreamed of meeting exotic women from faraway lands, disappears into a tent of belly dancers. Ed, the old football hero who lost an arm and a leg, sees himself whole in the House of Mirrors.

Miss Foley, the old spinster school marm who was one the most beautiful women in Greentown, becomes young and beautiful again. Young and beautiful and blind. It seems that all these gifts come with a price.

WILL HALLOWAY

A grown-up Will Halloway speaks of Greentown, the people who live there, and the perfect autumn day that Dark's Pandemonium Carnival came to town.

First of all, it was October; a rare month for boys. Full of cold winds— long nights—dark promises. The shadows lengthen. The wind mourns in such a way, you want to run forever through the fields because up ahead, the thousand pumpkins lie waiting to be cut. It was the October of my twelfth year, when the seller of lightning rods came along the road towards Greentown, Illinois, seeking glances over his shoulder. Somewhere, not far back, was a terrible storm. Even now, on those special autumn days, when the air smells like smoke, and the twilights are orange and ash gray, my mind goes back to Greentown, the place where I grew up. In my memory, I'm back on Main Street again among the neighbors who gave me my first glimpses into the fearful needs of the human heart. The cigar store was owned by Mr. Tetley; a man obsessed with money. Mr. Crosetti, our barber, cut my hair one thousand times; always talking about faraway ladies he would never know. I remember Ed, the barman. Yesterday's football hero, still haunted by forty-yard runs down the dark fields of his dreams. Our teacher was Miss Foley. We couldn't believe it but folks said that once, before we were even born, she had been the most beautiful woman in town. And of course I can still see Jim Nightshade; my best friend, my blood brother, my shadow. But I suppose that this is really the story of my father, and that strange leaf-whispery autumn when his heart was suddenly too old and too tired and too full of yearning and regrets, and he didn't know what to do about it.

MR. HALLOWAY

Will's father speaks of the day by the river when Will nearly drowned as he just sat and watched. He is filled with bitterness and shame for his weakness.

Well, about that picnic down by the Indigo River. Now you sit, son. Sit until it's finished; done with. This talk we were trying to have last night. This one we should have had a long time ago. 'Bout that strong old current that swept you way out in the middle of the river and I stood there and watched, tied to the riverbank; helpless, because I had a dad who didn't think it was right to teach boys to swim. Well, there was a man standing, drinking out of a stone bottle on the other side of the river, and he dove in after you. Dove in without even taking his boots off and pulled you out of danger. I guess you must have been all of four years old at the time. No one else knew who it was, but I did. It was Harry Nightshade's son. Your friend Jim's dad; a couple of years before he lit off across the seas and was never seen in this town again. Mr. Nightshade did your father's work. I can't forgive myself for that—or him either, I guess. Well, I'll tell you something, son. When you see the end of things coming close and staring at you, it's not what you've done that you regret—it's what you didn't do. And most of all, that afternoon at the river, there was nothing I could do. Well, blame my father. If you like, blame me. We've got to stop blaming sometime.

ALL OF ME

1984

Universal Studios
Screenplay by Phil Robinson
Directed by Carl Reiner
Produced by Phil Robinson

1 MONOLOGUE
Roger/Edwina

SETTING: Los Angeles, 1980s

Edwina Cutwater has everything that money can buy. She lives in an enormous mansion, dresses in the finest clothes, shops in the most expensive stores in the world, and has more money than Fort Knox. There's only one problem; Edwina has been bedridden since birth and is expected to die at any moment.

Roger Cobb is a junior partner in the prestigious law firm that handles the Cutwater estate. Roger is facing an early mid-life crisis. He'd much rather be playing guitar with his buddies in the jazz band than practicing law. Roger is sent to Edwina's house to handle a minor legal matter, and the two hit it off like oil and water.

Roger finds Edwina domineering and Edwina finds Roger disrespectful. When she tells Roger of her plan to have her soul transmigrated into the body of Terry, the beautiful young daughter of the stableman, Roger decides that she is crazy and leaves. The next day, Edwina has herself rolled into the law firm and demands that Roger be fired.

In the heat of the discussion, she dies. The Tibetan holy man, Praka Llasa, who is to perform the transmigration, immediately sends Edwina's soul into a special bowl that has been prepared to receive her spirit. The bowl accidently gets knocked out the window and lands on top of Roger's head.

Edwina's soul enters Roger, and the two must learn to get along in order to find Praka Llasa, Terry, and the bowl. As Edwina experiences life from within a healthy body, she gradually relaxes, and begins to enjoy herself.

Roger warms to Edwina, and the two become friends. As this comedy comes to a close, all parties are finally reunited and Edwina is transmigrated into Terry's body. Roger is then able to fulfill one of Edwina's oldest desires by dancing with her new body in the ballroom of the Cutwater Mansion.

ROGER/EDWINA

When Edwina's soul first enters Roger's body, there is a great deal of confusion. Roger thinks he's going crazy until he realizes what has happened. As it happens, Edwina now controls one half of his body. The two struggle to move Roger down the street and into his office—arguing all the way. (Edwina's lines are in parenthesis.)

(Where am I?) What? (I'm breathing! I must be alive!) Who said that? (No, I can't be. I just died.) I'm picking up "General Hospital" in my fillings! (Then it worked! Oh, my lord!) What the hell is happening to me? (I feel like the healthiest woman alive!) Who said that? (I did.) I'm going crazy! (Uh-oh. That does not sound like Fred's daughter.) No, I'm not going crazy. Something hit me on the head. I'm just hallucinating, that's all. (Oh, shit.) What the hell are you doing in there? (I can't believe this. I can't even die right.) Why are you doing this to me? (Dear God, aren't you getting enough laughs up there? What did I ever do to you?) Somebody please tell me that this is not happening. (I'm afraid it is, so let's just go inside and have Praka Llasa straighten out this mess.) Oh, Jeez, I can't move my right leg! I'm paralyzed! (Here, let me try. We obviously have mutual control over our body.) Our body? It's my body! I'm not sharing my body with anyone!

CRIMES OF PASSION

1984

New World Pictures
Screenplay by Barry Sandler
Directed by Ken Russell
Produced by Barry Sandler

1 MONOLOGUE
The Reverend Peter Shane

SETTING: An American city, 1980s

Crimes of Passion is a surreal glimpse into the dark world of sexual fantasy. Director Ken Russell has created a sensuous and dangerous backdrop of an inner-city red-light district in which to weave his tale of the failure of the American marriage.

Bobby, an average middle-class husband and father, moonlights for a detective agency to make ends meet. He is hired to follow Joanna, whose boss suspects her of selling company secrets. What Bobby finds out about Joanna is shocking, but it has nothing to do with company secrets. By day she is a sophisticated fabric designer; by night she becomes "China Blue," the most wanton and desirable hooker on the strip.

Facinated, Bobby—who cannot remember the last time he and his wife made love—knocks on China Blue's door and finds himself drawn helplessly into her world.

But Bobby isn't the only one watching China Blue's nocturnal rompings. The Reverend Peter Shane is a self-styled redeemer who has become so obsessed with China Blue that he now believes it is his sole mission in life to save her soul. The good Reverend's obsession leads to violence when he follows Joanna to her real home. The two struggle, and the Reverend produces the blue silk dress of China

Blue. Bobby arrives at Joanna's in time to hear her frightened scream. He breaks down the door to see China Blue slumped in the darkness. Without warning, the black-clothed figure of the Reverend leaps out of the darkness and stabs China Blue in the back.

Before Bobby can react, China Blue is revealed to be the Reverend, who has dressed in her outfit while forcing Joanna to wear his own minister's collar. In killing the image of China Blue, Joanna is finally able to leave the past behind while freeing the tortured spirit of the Reverend.

The film ends with both Joanna and Bobby facing an uncertain but possible future together.

THE REVEREND PETER SHANE

At the taut climax of the film, the Reverend confronts Joanna in her apartment. He reviles the spirit of China Blue and challenges her to seek salvation.

No more deceptions, Joanna. I know who you are. We're the same, don't you see? The same rage, the same fear. We hurt the same. We escape the same. But, we don't have to anymore. We have a chance, both of us, together. No more disguises. I'm crying out to you, for God's sake! Is everything a negotiation here, too? Listen to me, help me! I'm tired of standing on street corners. I want to love, and care, and need—just like you do. We could help each other. We don't have to grow old at all! It's all right, Joanna. Run away—turn on me. I was only trying to save you. Well, the game's not over. The messenger of God will return and this time he'll bring the final word. Last rites. Lovely apartment. What do you call it, Paradise Lost? The Reverend is going to save you tonight, once and for all. Don't fight me, child. I'm the messenger of God and I only want to heal you. You're opposing me, Joanna. You have to trust me. One more game— the final one—will free you forever. Do I have your trust? Because I can only play if I have your trust. Do I have it? Now, listen to me! I want your trust and I'm going to have it in any way I can. Now, you will follow the Reverend's orders, is that clear? Good. Now, I believe you'll find this game unique. It's one you've never played before and never will again, so make the most of it. It's known as "Exorcizing the Demons." In my calling it's the ultimate salvation and its ends are sacrosanct. With my ecclesiastic gift plus the grace of God and a little help from Superman here, I shall bestow upon you the supreme humanitarian blessing and give you your freedom. You do want that, don't you? I knew you would. Why? My mission has always been your salvation, but you trusted me, you refused to see. But I saw. I looked at you and I saw myself. I saw the same escape, the same malignancy. But I know the cure and I know how desperately you need it—and only I can give it to you. I want to, Joanna. Because it's my gift to you: freedom. It's the only thing I have left to give. You refused it once, but this time you have no choice. Getting into the part, my love? I know I am. Remember, scumbag, I'm here for your benefit, got that? Healthy looking plants. You must water them diligently. I've always preferred plastic flowers, myself. I could never bear to watch the real ones die. That's the trouble with living things, I suppose: inevitably they die. You've never seen anybody die, have you? Certainly not up close. That swift final gasp and then absolute silence. The stillness of the body as the flesh turns white. You're terrified right now because you think of it as death, but think of it as freedom.

UNDER THE VOLCANO

1984

Universal Studios
Screenplay by Guy Gallo
Based on the novel by Malcolm Lowry
Directed by John Huston
Produced by Moritz Borman

1 MONOLOGUE
Geoffrey Firmin

SETTING: Mexico, late 1930s

Geoffrey Firmin is a man tormented by the past in this dark tale of one man's descent into hell on earth. Firmin is a former British ambassador to Mexico, where he has chosen to live out his life. A slave to alcohol, Firmin's drinking has cost him his wife, Yvonne, who has left him to find a new life for herself in America.

When the story begins, Firmin is living a profligate existence in the small Mexican town he has made his home. Joined in his nightly revelry by his good friend and fellow alcoholic, the town doctor, the ex-ambassador finds himself sinking deeper and deeper into the folds of inebriety. No longer able to distinguish between fantasy and re-ality, past and present, day and night, Firmin's life has become a living hell.

Yvonne returns to this nightmare without warning, determined to give her husband one final chance. Her arrival manages to shock Firmin briefly from his dark reverie, and he makes a final and pa-thetic effort to stay sober.

The story reaches its climax on the Day of the Dead, one of Mexico's biggest holidays and a day that holds much fascination for Firmin. He, Yvonne, and his younger brother travel to a nearby town

for the celebration. Firmin is unable to resist the temptation of alcohol, and he staggers off, drunk, into the crowd. He makes his way
to a whorehouse outside of town that has a bad reputation and a
worse clientele. The locals become convinced that Firmin is a spy
and kill him. Yvonne arrives at the scene moments later only to be
killed herself by a bolting horse.

GEOFFREY FIRMIN

While attending a Red Cross Ball, Geoffrey accosts a German diplomat
with a drunken tirade about the Mexican train system.

Yes, quite. The Munich Pact and all that. Peace in our time—but
let's not be too hasty! Let's hedge our bets, what? After all, the
Mexican railroad has! They don't mean to be taken by surprise. Just
take a look at their newest timetable—at the fine print. Corpses must
be transported by express. Each of these express corpses must be
accompanied by a first-class passenger. Now let's suppose the Treaty
fails and it's bloody armageddon. Just think. We stand to make a
fortune! But just think of it! All those bloody corpses, each holding
a first-class ticket. One Day of the Dead won't be enough! Month,
Decade, Age of the Dead, more like. The whole world will learn to
laugh at the sight of stinking cadavers. Ha ha, bloody ha ha ha. Oh,
God: express trains will be booked up years in advance! Corpses hand
in hand with bloody first-class ticket holders standing in lines for
miles waiting for transport. Ladies and Gentlemen of the Red Cross,
you have your bloody work cut out for you!

BIRDY

1985

Tri Star Pictures
Written by Sandy Kroopf and Jack Behr
Based on the novel by William Wharton
Directed by Alan Parker
Produced by Alan Marshall

1 MONOLOGUE
Al

SETTING: An army mental hospital during the Vietnam conflict.

Al and Birdy are best friends. They grew up in the same Philadelphia neighborhood together, enjoying the short-lived innocence of the 50s. Now they have both returned from Vietnam, and each is drastically changed.

Al Columbato is summoned to an army mental hospital to see his friend Birdy. Al was sent home after losing half of his face when he stepped on a mine, and the doctor in charge of Birdy's case thinks the recuperating Al can help his friend to break out of a catatonic state brought on by something that happened in Vietnam.

Birdy squats in the corner of his hospital room, giving no sign of recognizing his old friend. Al sits on the bed and begins to talk about the years they spent together in Philadelphia, and so begins a sojourn that will eventually take them both through a series of emotional remembrances.

Flashbacks to their high school years reveal Al as a handsome young man filled with a lust for life who befriends the shy Birdy, whose only desire is to fly. This desire turns to obsession over the years as Birdy gradually begins to mentally metamorphose into a bird.

Unable to cope with his friend's detachment, Al gives up and enlists for Vietnam. Birdy watches, broken-hearted, as Al leaves for battle. Now Al has a second chance to save his friend.

AL

At the film's climax, Al holds Birdy in his arms as he speaks about his fears for both of them. Al is frightened of having his bandages removed and seeing what his new face looks like. He feels destroyed by the war. Since he has been unable to reach Birdy, he now feels that his only salvation is to become crazy like his friend.

Don't worry, Birdy. I'm not leaving you again. They can't make me leave you. I can't go out there. I couldn't make it. They got the best of us, Birdy. We're both totally screwed-up. I mean, we haven't had anything to do with making our own lives. Fuck! I was always so damn sure about being myself and how nobody was going to make me do anything I didn't want. And now, here I am. Finish you off with a discharge or put you on a casualty list. It doesn't matter how special you are or were. I feel like one of those dogs nobody wanted. Remember. You know, when that shell went off in my face, I could smell burning flesh and it was crazy because the smell was so sweet; so familiar. And then I realized it was my own flesh that was burning. And I couldn't even touch the pain. I don't even know what I look like anymore, Birdy. I don't know if it's me under these bandages or what some army meat-cutter thinks is me. Jesus Christ, I don't want a patched up instant pity excuse for a face! I just want it to be Al under here. Not some sewn together freak mask. Shit! What's so great about their fucking world anyway? We'll just stay here and stay the hell out of it. I don't have to get these bandages off. You see, I figured out what you're doing, Birdy. You're right, we should just hide out and not talk with anybody. And every so often go crazy and up the wall, and spit, and throw shit at them like the looney hall. Yeah, that's what we can do. That's what we can

THE COCA-COLA K.

1985

Cinecom International Films
Screenplay by Frank Moorhouse
Directed by Dusan Makavejev
Produced by David Roe

1 MONOLOGUE
Becker

SETTING: Sydney, Australia, 1980s

The Coca-Cola Kid is a comedy from down-under in search of love, corporate values, and the perfect Australian sound. Becker, an ex–U.S. Marine turned marketing genius, is sent by the Coca-Cola Company to Australia to troubleshoot the local soft-drink industry.

He is warily received at Coca-Cola's Sydney headquarters, where he finds none of the hard-driving dedication so typical of American corporations. His killer instinct is a mere curiosity to his Australian counterparts who enjoy a far more relaxed pace of life. Indeed, the straight-laced Becker is baffled by everyone he encounters; from Teri, his sexy secretary, to T. George McDowell, a crusty old soft-drink magnate who happens to control a valley that sells little to no Coke. McDowell makes his own pop in an antiquated steam-powered bottling plant, and the people for miles around are loyal to his products. Becker is determined to buy out T. George, but the old man refuses his offer. Despite himself, Becker grows to admire and respect T. George. He also falls in love with Teri, who turns out to be T. George's estranged daughter.

The story reaches its climax when T. George, his back against the wall and no longer able to fend off Becker's corporate onslaught, blows up his bottling plant. A shocked Becker realizes that he can

be a part of the machine that has brought about the de-
of such a wonderful man. He turns his company credit cards
oes to Teri, who welcomes him gladly. Becker is no longer
er in a strange land.

BECKER

*e ex-Marine addresses the administrative staff at Coca-Cola in Sydney
r the first time. He speaks as would a southern revivalist preacher to his
ock: filled with fire and confidence. His audience has never seen or heard
anything like him before.*

You may be asking yourselves, what is an ex-Marine doing on this
side of the globe? Well, Marines fall on every continent on the face
of the earth except Australia, so here I am. First, we have to ask
ourselves: Do we need to explain our product to the public? Last year
in Rome I had an opportunity to talk to one of the top guys in the
Jesuit heirarchy and he told me, he said, they consider us—excuse
me miss, your feet belong on the floor—they consider us in bringing
God's business of good will and good news to the people no less than
second to themselves in this whole wide God-fearing world, yes.
They see us as the smart guys who distribute and sell the miracle of
America. And that's exactly what we are. When you have a product
with charisma, you don't have to explain a God damn thing. No.
You need only bring it to the people. Try to analyze it and you'll
come up with: dark color, cold, wet, and bubbly. Come on, that is
no way to explain what getting in touch with the American way of
life really means to billions of people. Listen—the sound of Coke.
Dark and bubbly. Why our dark and bubbly liquid is so loved by all
those Eskimos and other Canadians we don't need to know. We need
only to bring it to the people.

CREATOR

1985

Screenplay by Jeremy Leven
Based on the book by Jeremy Leven
Directed by Ivan Passer
Produced by Stephen Friedman

1 MONOLOGUE
Boris

SETTING: An American university, the present

Dr. Harry Wolper is a genius. A Nobel laureate employed as Chairman of the School of Medicine at a large university, Harry has found the perfect playground for his experimentation with genetics. Harry is trying to grow Lucy, his dead wife with whom he is still very much in love, in his laboratory from cells he has saved since her death.

Harry and Boris, the young graduate student whom Harry has hired to assist him with his secret project, have grown very close. Boris turns to his mentor for insight into life, and when he falls in love with the beautiful Barbara, Harry offers sage advice concerning affairs of the heart.

Suddenly, Barbara collapses with a rare illness that puts her in a coma. Her parents want the hospital to shut down Barbara's life support, but Harry intervenes, giving Boris forty-eight hours to talk her out of the coma. Boris uses the entire forty-eight hours, talking until he is hoarse and near collapse himself. Just as the life support is about to be disconnected, Barbara awakens. Boris knows that he owes this miracle to Harry's unending faith in life.

BORIS

ris speaks to the comatose Barbara in a desperate attempt to save her. e tearfully pleads with her to give the doctors any kind of sign that she still alive, and is finally rewarded when she grabs his hand.

I'm scared, Barbara. I get really scared sometimes. The first time I asked you to move in with me I was scared. The first time we made love I was scared. Barbara, I wish we could go home. You know, you make me feel better. God, Barbara, I couldn't stand it if you died. You know I need you a lot, Barbara. I mean, there are so many things I want to do with you, and if I don't get a chance to do them, I'm going to be really heartbroken. Barbara, please, Barbara—you've got to do something to show them you're alive. You've got to do something. You've got to show them. You gotta do it for me, Barbara. Please, just show them. Just help me, Barbara. I need you, Barbara. Please, help me, Barbara. For me, do it for me, Barbara. Barbara, please help me! You gotta do it! You can do it! Show them, Barbara. Please, help me, Barbara! Sid! She's grabbing my hand! Sid! She's crying! She's alive! Barbara's alive! Look, Sid! Barbara!

KISS OF THE SPIDER WOMAN

1985

Screenplay by Leonard Schrader
Based on the novel by Manuel Puig
Directed by Hector Babenco
Produced by David Weisman

2 MONOLOGUES
Molina
Valentin

SETTING: A prison in an unnamed South American country in the 1980s.

Kiss of the Spider Woman is the haunting story of two men unjustly imprisoned by a brutal South American junta. Based on the best-selling novel by Manuel Puig, *Kiss of the Spider Woman* is the tale of Molina, a gentle man imprisoned for his homosexuality, and of Valentin, member of an underground political organization determined to free the people of his country.

Forced to share a cell, these two very different men learn to come to terms with one another. Valentin learns that there is more to being a man than biological determination, and Molina learns that there are things in life worth giving your life for.

To escape the hellish nightmare of prison, Molina likes to "tell" his favorite movie. In this way the two men are able to leave the pain and humiliation of torture behind, if only for a few moments, as they enter the beautiful fantasy world of Molina's imagination. When the two men finally part, they have forged a love that transcends politics and sexuality.

MOLINA

Molina bitterly speaks of his life outside prison and of the terrible loneliness that preys upon his soul. He describes meeting what he likes to call a "real man" and of his frustrated feelings of love.

I'll cry about whatever I want to. Do you think you're the only one who's suffered? Do you think it's easy to find a real man? One who is humble and yet has dignity. How many years have I been searching; how many nights; how many faces filled with scorn and deceit? I mean, you know, working as a window-dresser—enjoyable as it is— sometimes at the end of the day you wonder what it's all about. You feel kind of empty inside. Then, one night, my heart was pounding; so afraid that I would get hurt once again. His white tunic, the way he moved, his sad smile; everything seemed so perfect, like in the movies. You have no idea how much trouble I went through, month after month, just to get him to go for a walk. But little by little, I made him see that I respected him. Anyway, after more than a year, we finally became friends. Nothing at all happened—ever. Don't you know anything at all? He's straight, he's married. I said to him: "Just once. Let's do it just once." But he never wanted to.

VALENTIN

Here, Valentin describes Marta, the woman he loves. He tells of the day that he told her about his subversive activities and of the events which led to his arrest. He verbally denounces his martyrdom and pleads for life.

I'm going to tell you the truth. During torture, whenever I felt close to death, it was Marta I would think about and she would save me. My whole body ached to hold her. She's upper-class; pure bourgeoi- sie. She's got everything; money, looks, education, freedom. I'm such a hypocrite. Just like all those class-conscious pigs. I must admit, it was convenient; a safe place to stay when I was forced to hide. Until one day I had to tell her about my other life. She just listened in silence like she knew already. Then she asked me to leave the movement. But how could I do nothing when my friends were disappearing every day? I sensed that she was right, but I had no choice. So once again I didn't know what to say. I no longer believed in violence, but I had to do something. As a journalist, I was always hearing about the illegal arrests and secret torture, then leaking this information abroad. My assignment was to meet one of the last surviving members of the original movement. His code name was "Dr. Amerigo." He needed my passport to leave the country. He had accomplished almost nothing, but I was glad I could help him. I don't deserve to die in this cell. I only confessed some code names they already knew. I can't stand being a martyr. It infuriates me. I don't want to be a martyr. My whole life is a mistake. Give me your hand. I don't want to die, Molina. I don't want to die.

OUT OF AFRICA

1985

Universal Pictures
Screenplay by Kurt Luedtke
Based on the memoir by Isak Dinesen
Directed by Sidney Pollack
Produced by Sidney Pollack

4 MONOLOGUES
Karen 1
Karen 2
Karen 3
Karen 4

SETTING: Kenya, after 1914

Isak Dinesen traveled to Kenya in 1914 to live on her husband's coffee plantation. *Out of Africa* is a collection of her remembrances of that time in her life.

Deserted by her irresponsible and unfaithful husband the Baron von Blixen, Karen must somehow manage the failing plantation and cope with living alone in a land so different form her native Denmark. Despite many hardships, Karen falls in love with the land and the people of Kenya. She also falls in love with Denys Finch Hatton, a British adventurer who teaches her the importance of personal freedom.

Karen's time in Africa and with Denys are both cut tragically short when her plantation fails and Denys is killed in a plane crash. She buries Denys high on a hill overlooking the land that they had both come to cherish and then returns to Denmark where she will eventually turn her remembrances of Africa into some of the world's best-loved literature.

KAREN 1

An older Karen now living in Denmark remembers Denys and Kenya. Her pain in remembering is evident.

He was an animal who loved Mozart . . . instinctively, without the need to know that it *was* Mozart . . . He began our friendship with a gift. It was the day after we met. And later, not long before Tsavo, he gave me another, incredible gift: a glimpse of the world through God's eye! And I thought: Yes, I see . . . this is the way it was intended. I've written about all the others, not because I loved them less, but because they were clearer . . . easier. He was waiting for me there. But I've gone ahead of my story. He hated that. Denys loved to hear a story told well. You see . . . I had a farm in Africa at the foot of the Ngong Hills . . .

KAREN 2

Karen speaks of her time with Denys, remembering ordinary events as if they were miracles.

The friends of the farm came to the house and went away again. They were not the kind of people who stay for a long time in the same place. Neither were they the kind who grow old. But they had sat contented by the fire, and when the house, closing round them, said: "I will not let thee go except thou bless me," they laughed and blessed it, and it let them go. In the days and hours that Denys was at home, we spoke of nothing ordinary, not of my troubles with the farm or of his with his work—or of anything at all that was small, and real. We lived disconnected and apart from things. I had been making up stories while he was away. In the evenings he made himself comfortable, spreading cushions like a couch in front of the fire—and with me sitting on the floor, cross-legged like Scheherazade herself, he would listen, clear-eyed, to a long tale, from where it began to where it ended.

KAREN 3

Her plantation has failed, and Karen must return to Denmark. This monologue is a eulogy of loss.

If I know a song of Africa, of the giraffe and the African new moon lying on her back, of the plows in the fields and the sweaty faces of the coffee pickers, does Africa know a song of me? Will the air over the plain quiver with a color that I have had on, or the children invent a game in which my name is, or the full moon throw a shadow over the gravel of the drive that was like me, or will the eagles of the Ngong Hills look out for me?

KAREN 4

Denys has been killed in an airplane crash. A softly grieving Karen speaks of the lions that are said to sleep on his grave.

The mail has come today, and a friend writes this to me: The Masai have reported to the district commissioner at Ngong that many times, at sunrise and sunset, they have seen lions on Finch Hatton's grave. A lion and a lioness have come there, and stood, or lain, on the grave for a long time. After you went away, the ground round the grave leveled out into a sort of terrace. I suppose that the level place makes a good site for the lions. From there, they can have a view over the plain, and the cattle and game on it. Denys will like that: I must remember to tell him.

THE SURE THING

1985

Embassy Films Associates
Presents a Monument Pictures Production of a
Rob Reiner Film
Screenplay by Steven L. Broom and Jonathan Roberts
Directed by Rob Reiner
Produced by Roger Birnbaum

1 MONOLOGUE
Gib

SETTING: A New England college, the present

Gib is a freshman at a college in New England. His best friend, Lance, attends school in southern California, and begs Gib to come out for the Christmas holidays. He sends Gib a photo of a gorgeous blonde in a bikini and assures him that she is a "sure thing."

Alison is a classmate of Gib's and his antithesis in nature. Where Gib is spontaneous and charming, Alison is repressed and cold. Imagine their discomfort when they find themselves crammed in the back seat of an old Volvo stationwagon sharing a ride to Los Angeles. Their constant bickering pushes the car's driver over the edge and they find themselves booted out of the car in the middle of the vast and empty American plains.

Gib and Alison must learn to cooperate, pooling their resources in order to make it to California. They fall in love on the way, but when Alison overhears Gib telling a truck driver who has given them a lift about the "sure thing" waiting for him in L.A., she becomes furious and storms off as soon as they reach the city.

When college resumes, Alison and Gib's writing teacher reads Gib's latest short story aloud in class. It tells the story of his encounter with the "sure thing" and how he turned her down. As Gib takes much ribbing from his male classmates for having turned down such an offer, he and Alison find one another, knowing that they have both finally found a sure thing.

GIB

At the beginning of the film, Gib tries to persuade the rigid Alison to tutor him in English. He chases her up and down the pool as she swims laps, painting a grim picture of his future life should he flunk out of college.

I'm flunking English and I was wondering if you would help me. If I flunk English, I'm outta here. I can kiss college good-bye. I don't know what I'll do. I'll probably go home. Gee, Dad'll be pissed off, Mom will be heartbroken, and if I play my cards right, I get—maybe— a six-month grace period and then I gotta get a job and you know what that means. That's right. They start me off at the drive-up window and I gradually work my way from shakes to burgers. And then, one day my lucky break comes. The french-fry guy dies and they offer me the job. But, the day I'm supposed to start, some men come by in a black Lincoln Continental and tell me I can make a quick three hundred just for driving a van back from Mexico. When I get out of jail, I'm thirty-six years old, living in a flop house—no job, no home, no upward mobility, very few teeth. And then, one day, they find me; face down, talking to the gutter, clutching a bottle of paint thinner. And why? Because you wouldn't help me in English! No, you were too busy to help a drowning man!

DESERT BLOOM

1986

Columbia Pictures
Screenplay by Eugene Corr
Directed by Eugene Corr
Produced by Michael Hausman

3 MONOLOGUES
Rose
Jack 1
Jack 2

SETTING: Las Vegas, Nevada, 1950

This family drama centers around the Chismores of Las Vegas and their experiences during the year of "A" Bomb testing in the Nevada desert. Rose Chismore, a sensitive and attractive young girl, comes of age in the shadow of the impending atomic explosion. In a town gone "bomb-crazy," Rose struggles to come to terms with Jack, her abusive and alcoholic stepfather, a WWII vet who lives in a dark fantasy world of his own design; Lilly, her hardworking mother, a woman with a taste for gambling; and Starr, Lilly's sensual sister who is staying with the Chismores while she awaits her divorce. Rose is drawn into this triangle against her will and her journey takes her into the desert on the night before the detonation. As the family gathers to watch the mushroom cloud blossom in the gray Nevada sky, Rose learns the most important lesson of all: How to forgive.

ROSE

An older Rose remembers Las Vegas as it was in 1950. She recalls getting her first pair of glasses, and how they made the town look completely different.

When I was six years old, my grandmother took us out to the desert to look for wildflowers. Just where you'd think nothing in the world could grow, that's where they were. Grandma told us that those were her favorites. The ones that could grow in the hardest places. I was nine when mama married Jack. We were always moving after that. One desert town after another. And so I saved things. Remembering was my way of making things matter. Las Vegas was a small desert town in 1950. There was nothing but some hotels, and casinos, and the airforce base. I knew every inch of it, but my glasses made everything look different; including, I hoped, me. I had a theory that glasses would make me look like Ingrid Bergman. Vegas is a glamorous town, and with my glasses, I thought I fit right in. I loved movies, books, Wonder Woman, and my grandmother. Real life was another matter. That year my stepfather had a gas station on the edge of town. The last stop before four hundred miles of desert. We were at war in Korea and the town was filling up with thousands of men in suits and uniforms; all headed out to the desert. No one knew why they came or what they were doing. I felt the glasses gave me mystery and cheekbones. . . .

JACK 1

Jack recounts his WWII experiences for the young boy who helps out in his garage. This is his favorite fantasy and he revels in a willing audience.

Patton was the best. He drove right by me in his jeep once. "Georgie," we called him. I said, "It's okay, boys; Georgie's here!" He got out and walked right next to me. BS-ed like a regular guy; Patton. Jesus, it was cold. The Germans had the 101st pinned down at Bastone. If they break through they might win the war. Fifty miles a day we made through snow up to our waist. Supply had to parachute in our gas and ammo we moved so fast. No army ever moved like the Third. Krauts thought we were the Dogs of Hell. French girls . . . well, you're too young for that. It's history. We caught the Germans at Bastone, we stopped them. When they asked us to surrender we told them, "Nuts." It was our greatest moment. Now the commies have taken everything, anyway. Everything we fought for. . . .

JACK 2

In a rare moment, Jack speaks candidly with Rose about the night he married her mother.

Duke Ellington. He's the greatest composer since Beethoven and he's a nigger . . . negro. Here, listen. It's the only thing in the world that matters right there. Even if the commies take over. You don't believe me, do you? What I said about things being different. That's okay. You don't know what I can do when I set my mind to it. The night I married your mother you hit me over the head with a frying pan. Some honeymoon. Little nine-year-old girl had to climb up on a chair to hit her stepfather over the head with a fryin' pan. Sort of got us off on the wrong foot, didn't it? It took guts, I like that. You didn't understand. You thought you were protecting your mother. That's what I'm trying to do. Protect my family. Well, no hard feelings.

HANNAH AND HER SISTERS

1986

Orion
Screenplay by Woody Allen
Directed by Woody Allen
Produced by Roger Greenhut

3 MONOLOGUES
Elliot
Holly
Mickey

SETTING: Manhattan, 1980s

Hannah is a once-successful actress who has given up her career and is now happily married to Elliot, a Manhattan businessman who happens to be experiencing a mid-life crisis.

Hannah's sisters, Holly and Leigh, face personal crises of their own. Holly is frustrated after years of auditioning for Broadway shows and never getting cast; and Leigh is facing the end of a live-in relationship with a brooding artist.

Elliot has become obsessed with Leigh, who returns his feelings of passion. Their short affair threatens to tear unwitting Hannah's life apart.

Meanwhile, Holly has begun to date Mickey, Hannah's hypochondriacal ex-husband, who is always convinced that he is dying from some strange ailment or other. As time goes by, Leigh ends her affair with Elliot, who reacts with nothing short of relief. He now realizes that this love for Hannah and their children is stronger than his brief passion for Leigh. Holly abandons her acting career and turns to writing. She and Mickey finally marry. Hannah has been the rock to which they have all clung during this turbulent time, and as the story ends, she serves them all yet another Thanksgiving dinner.

ELLIOT

Elliot lusts after Leigh as he watches her move around his apartment during a Thanksgiving gathering.

God, she's beautiful. She's got the prettiest eyes, and she looks so sexy in that sweater. I just want to be alone with her and hold her and kiss her and tell her how much I love her and take care of her . . . stop it, you idiot; she's your wife's sister. I can't help it. I'm consumed by her. It's been months now. I dream about her. I think about her at the office. Oh, Leigh, what am I going to do? I hear myself mooning over you and it's disgusting. Before, when she squeezed past me in the doorway, and I smelled that perfume on the back of her neck—Jesus, I thought I was going to swoon. Easy, you're a dignified financial advisor. It doesn't look good for you to swoon.

HOLLY

After meeting a handsome and eligible man, Holly finds herself sitting in the back seat of his car while her best friend April rides in front. She bemoans the fact that he is more interested in April.

Naturally, I get taken home first. Well, obviously he prefers April. Of course, I was so tongue-tied all night. I can't believe I said that about the Guggenheim: my stupid little roller skating joke. I should never tell jokes. Mom can tell them; and Hannah, but I kill them. Where did April come up with that stuff about Adolph Loos and terms like "organic form"? Well naturally, she went to Brandeis. But I don't think she knows what she's talking about. Could you believe the way she was calling him David? "Yes, David. I feel that way, too, David. What a marvelous space, David." I hate April. She's pushy. Now they'll drop me and she'll invite him up. I blew it. And I really like him alot! Oh, screw it. I'm not going to get all upset. I've got reading to do tonight. Maybe I'll get into bed early. I'll turn on a movie and take an extra Seconal.

MICKEY

Mickey, the likable yet paranoid hypochondriac, awaits the results of yet another medical test, convincing himself that he is dying.

Okay, take it easy. He didn't say you had anything—he just doesn't like the spot in your X-ray, that's all. Doesn't mean you have anything. Don't jump to conclusions. Nothing's going to happen to you. You're in the middle of New York City; this is your town. You're surrounded by people and traffic and restaurants. God, how can you just one day vanish? Keep calm. You're going to be okay. Don't panic. I'm dying, I'm dying! I know it! There's a spot on my lung! All right now, take it easy, will ya? It's not on your lung—it's on your ear. It's the same thing, isn't it? Oh, Jeez—I can't sleep. Oh, God, there's a tumor in my head the size of a basketball! Now I keep thinking: I can feel it every time I blink. Oh, Jesus! He wants to do a brain scan to confirm what he already suspects. Look, I'll make a deal with God: let it be my ear, okay? I'll go deaf. I'll go deaf and blind in one eye, maybe. But I don't want a brain operation. Once they go into my skull I'll wind up like the guy with the wool cap who delivers for the florist. Oh, relax, will you? Your whole life you run to doctors—the news is always fine. That's not true. What about years ago?

THE MOSQUITO COAST

1986

Warner Brothers
Screenplay by Paul Schraeder
Based on the novel by Paul Theroux
Directed by Peter Weir
Produced by Jerome Hellman

2 MONOLOGUES
Allie 1
Allie 2

SETTING: The fictional country of Mosquitia located in Central America, 1980s

The Mosquito Coast is the haunting tale of one man's obsessive desire to make a perfect world for himself and his family in a remote jungle village in the mythical country of Mosquitia. Inventor Allie Fox is disenchanted with the American Dream. Frustrated by the lack of American-made goods and the deteriorating quality of life, the eccentric Allie longs to expatriate. On a whim, he moves his wife and four small children to the Central American jungles of Mosquitia. Determined to master his environment, Allie dedicates himself to carving out a utopian society from the ceaseless jungle-growth only to find that the jungle can have no master. His obsession leads to madness, and a scuffle with an American fundamentalist missionary leaves him fatally wounded. The Foxes then find themselves cast adrift on a raft with no food or water; their only salvation to be found in the impending death of the tyrannical Allie.

ALLIE 1

Allie reviles America in this near-fevered speech to his oldest son, Charlie, while shopping in a hardware store. People stare as he speaks, non-stop, of his nightmare vision of America.

Look around you. How did America get this way? Land of promise, land of opportunity. Give us the wretched refuse of your teeming shores. Have a Coke, watch TV. Go on welfare, get free money. Turn to crime; crime pays in this country. Why do they keep coming? Look around you, Charlie. This place is a toilet. The whole damn country has turned into a dope-taking, door-locking, ulcerated danger zone. Rabid scavengers, criminal millionaires, moral sneaks. Nobody ever thinks of leaving this country. I do. I think about it every day. I'm the last man. I want an eight-foot length of rubber seal with foam backing. This country's going to the dogs. Nobody cares. "I just work here," that's the attitude. Buy junk, sell junk, eat junk. Who are you working for? The Japanese? Look, "Made in Japan." I don't want my hard-earned American dollars converted into yen. I want an American length of rubber seal. Do you work here? All right, we'll get it someplace else. This is not the only place in town. Good bye, or maybe I should have said, "sayonara."

ALLIE 2

The inventor here explains to his family why he had to leave America as they huddle in a tent on their first night in the jungle. They still believe in him and are determined to make his dream a reality.

No one loves America more than I do, you know. That's why we left. Because I couldn't bear to watch. You kids have got to understand this. It's like when my mother died. She'd been strong as an ox—fell down, broke her hip, went into the hospital, and caught double pneunomia. She's lying in bed, dying. I went over and held her hand. She looked up at me and you know what she said? "Why don't you give me some rat poison?" Couldn't listen. Couldn't watch. So I went away. People said I was the height of callousness—it's not true. I loved her too much to watch her die.

PLATOON

1986

Hemdale Film Corporation
Screenplay by Oliver Stone
Directed by Oliver Stone
Produced by Arnold Kopelson

4 MONOLOGUES
Chris 1
Chris 2
Rhah
Elias

SETTING: Vietnam, somewhere near the Cambodian Border, 1967

Platoon is Oliver Stone's semi-autobiographical tale of his experiences in Vietnam. The three central characters of the story are Chris, an inexperienced nineteen-year-old who joins the seasoned platoon upon arrival in Vietnam; Sgt. Barnes, a man whose soul has been corrupted by the horrors of war; and Sgt. Elias, a man whose inner strength and courage withstand the hellish nightmare of Vietnam.

The film follows the platoon's progress through the jungle as they search for N.V.A. sympathizers and weapons caches. When they arrive in a village that they have been ordered to search, fear, rage, and bloodlust drive the men to commit atrocities. Chris is shocked by the platoon's actions which are capped by Barnes's cold-blooded murder of an old woman. Enraged, Elias attacks Barnes and the hatred between the two men is confirmed.

The next day, the platoon is attacked in the jungle. Separated from the rest of the men, Barnes seizes an opportunity to kill Elias. He tells Chris that Elias is dead when the choppers arrive to lift them out. As the chopper takes off, Elias stumbles out of the jungle, streaked with blood, and Chris knows that Barnes is the one who shot him. His outrage builds until days later when he is presented with a similar opportunity to kill. Unblinking, Chris shoots and kills Barnes, his innocence forever lost to the jungles of Southeast Asia.

CHRIS 1

Chris tells his grandmother about his new life in Vietnam in letters written shortly after his arrival and explains his reasons for joining up.

Somebody once wrote Hell is the impossibility of Reason. That's what this place feels like. I hate it already and it's only been a week. Some goddamn week, Grandma . . . (*checking his raw blisters*) . . . the hardest thing I think I've ever done is go on point, three times this week—I don't even know what I'm doing. A gook could be standing three feet in front of me and I wouldn't know it, I'm so tired. We get up at five a.m., hump all day, camp around four or five p.m., dig foxhole, eat, then put out an all-night ambush or a three-man listening post in the jungle. It's scary 'cause nobody tells me how to do anything cause I'm new and nobody cares about the new guys, they don't even want to know your name. The unwritten rule is a new guy's life isn't worth as much 'cause he hasn't put his time in yet— and they say if you're gonna get killed in Nam it's better to get it in the first few weeks, the logic being: you don't suffer that much. I can believe that . . . If you're lucky you get to stay in the perimeter at night and then you pull a three-hour guard shift, so maybe you sleep three-four hours a night, but you don't really sleep . . . I don't think I can keep this up for a year, Grandma—I think I've made a big mistake coming here . . .

CHRIS 2

. . .'Course Mom and Dad didn't want me to come, they wanted me to be just like them—respectable, hard-working, making $200 a

week, a little house, a family. They drove me crazy with their goddamn world, Grandma, you know Mom; I don't want to be a white
boy on Wall Street, I don't want my whole life to be predetermined
by them . . . I guess I have always been sheltered and special, I just
want to be anonymous. Like everybody else. Do my share for my
country. Live up to what Grandpa did in the First World War and
Dad the Second. I know this is going to be *the* war of my generation.
Well here I am—anonymous all right, with guys nobody really cares
about—they come from the end of the line, most of 'em, small towns
you never heard of—Pulaski, Tennessee; Brandon, Mississippi; Pork
Bend, Utah; Wampum, Pennsylvania. Two years high school's about
it, maybe if they're lucky a job waiting for 'em back in a factory, but
most of 'em got nothing, they're poor, they're the unwanted of our
society, yet they're fighting for our society and our freedom and what
we call America, they're the bottom of the barrel—and they know
it, maybe that's why they call themselves 'grunts' cause a 'grunt' can
take it, can take anything. They're the backbone of this country,
Grandma, the best I've ever seen, the heart and soul—I've found it
finally, way down here in the mud—maybe from down here I can
start up again and be something I can be proud of, without having
to fake it, maybe . . . I can see something I don't yet see, learn
something I don't yet know . . . I miss you, I miss you very much,
tell Mom I miss her too—Chris.

RHAH

Rhah, a black soldier, angrily denounces civilian life and indicates that the
fight will never be over.

Baaa! Fuck it, they sold us out—so what! What'd you'all expect? Civilian life is phoney BULLSHIT man. They're ROBOTS man—watchin'
dopey television and drivin' dopey cars, and they fuck up, nobody
dies. That's all right, you keep fuckin' up, politicians keep lyin'.
Cause it don't really matter. Don't mean shit. So what! Whatcha
want—a parade! Fuck that too! No war time no grunt never got no

respect. Till he was dead—and even THEN! You're fighting for YOUR-SELF man! You're fighting for your SOUL, that's all. Remember that. And it's some goddamned battle too—if you'se a man, wrestle with that angel . . . Love and Hate—the whole shitbag show, that's the story then and now and it ain't hardly gonna change . . .

ELIAS

Elias shares a joint with Chris and explains why he thinks that America will lose the war.

. . . We been kicking other people's asses so long I guess it's time we got our own kicked. The only decent thing I can see coming out of here are the survivors—hundreds of thousands of guys like you, Taylor, going back to every little town in the country knowing something about what it's like to take a life and what that can do to a person's soul—twist it like Barnes and Bunny and make 'em sick inside and if you got any brains you gonna fight it the rest of your life cause it's cheap, killing is cheap, the cheapest thing I know, and when some drunk like O'Neill starts glorifying it, you're gonna puke all over him and when the politicians start selling you a used war all over again, you and your generation gonna say go fuck yourself 'cause you know, you've seen it, and when you know it, deep down there . . . you know it *till you die* . . . that's why the survivors remember. 'Cause the dead don't let 'em forget.

RIVER'S EDGE

1986

Hemdale Film Corporation
Screenplay by Neal Jimenez
Directed by Tim Hunter
Produced by Sara Pillsbury and Midge Sanford

3 MONOLOGUES
Feck
John 1
John 2

SETTING: Oregon, 1980s

This chilling film is based on the true story of an Oregon high school student who murdered his girlfriend and then bragged of his accomplishment to his friends. When John kills his girlfriend by the river, he feels alive and in control for the first time in his life. When he tells his friends what he has done, they all drive to the river to view the body. After several days, the police are finally notified of the crime and a manhunt for John ensues.

John finds temporary shelter at the home of Feck, an ex–motorcycle gang member who killed *his* girlfriend in a jealous rage and has been hiding from the police for years while he sells pot to kids.

The community is shocked by the callousness of their teenagers, who visited the dead body without turning in the killer. As the hunt for John intensifies, he and Feck drive to the river where they drink beer and talk about the women they've killed. Feck killed out of love, whereas John killed out of boredom. Realizing that John is a true sociopath, Feck shoots him and then leaves the river's edge to return to his own hellish world. He is soon caught and arrested, and the surviving teens are left to wonder about their values and their lives.

FECK

The one-legged fugitive describes the motorcycle accident in which he lost his leg.

Motorcycle accident. The whole gang ditched me and kept on riding. My leg was right out in the middle of the street. I remember lying in the gutter, all bleeding and shaking; staring at my leg right next to a beer can. And I remember thinking, "That's my leg. I wonder if there's any beer in that can?" I also remember thinking, "Maybe they can sew that leg back on." And then there comes the ambulance and runs right over all of it. What'd I need it for, huh? I got another one, right?

JOHN 1

In the same conversation, John reveals his nihilistic nature as he tells Feck what happens when he starts fighting.

I figure when you start fighting you're always defending yourself. Me, I get in a fight—I go fucking crazy, you know? Everything goes black and then I fucking explode, you know? Like, it's the end of the world. And who cares if this guy wastes me 'cause I'm going waste him first. I mean, the whole world's gonna blow up anyway. I might as well keep my pride. I got this philosophy: You do shit, and it's done, and then you die. You got any more beer?

JOHN 2

As Feck and John sit by the river's edge, the young killer describes the feelings of power and control that he experienced when he strangled his girlfriend.

Come on, Feck! I'm with you. I killed a girl, too. Wanted to show the world who's boss. I didn't need no gun. I did mine with my hands. I was right there; I was right on top of her; I was face to face. I wasn't even mad, really. She didn't look too surprised, just a little stoned. After a few minutes her face puffed out and it turned dark purple and she just stared at me. She couldn't move, she couldn't scream. I had total control of her. I had total control of her. It all felt so real. It felt so real. She was dead, there in front of me and I felt so fucking alive! Is that how you felt, Feck? Funny thing is: I'm dead now. They're gonna fry me for sure.

SALVADOR

1986

A Greenberg Brothers Partnership
Screenplay by Oliver Stone and Richard Boyle
Directed by Oliver Stone
Produced by Gerald Green and Oliver Stone

2 MONOLOGUES
Major Max
Archbishop Romero

SETTING: El Salvador, 1980-82

The story of *Salvador* is taken from the true life experiences of photo-journalist Richard Boyle, who covered the civil wars in Nicaragua and El Salvador for NBC and CNN. Boyle is a hard-drinking, fast-talking con artist with a nose for news. He and his friend Doc, an out of work DJ, drive to El Salvador—worming their way past road blocks manned by death squads—to cover the action that Boyle knows is about to happen. In San Salvador we are introduced to a huge cast of characters including nuns, human rights activists, tor-turers, American embassy personnel, network journalists, and Major Max—the ruthless leader of the Nazi-like Arena Party responsible for the murder of Archbishop Romero.

The plight of the people is made clear as the heinous acts of the death squads are seen through the impartial eyes of the journalists. Boyle's Salvadoran lover, Maria, is in grave danger of being arrested because she lacks the necessary papers that allow safe passage. Boyle becomes determined to get Maria and her children out of the coun-try, and in a desperate attempt actually manages to get them across the border at Nogales. Their bus is stopped by immigration officers, however, and Maria and the children are taken away despite Boyle's frantic efforts to convince the officers that she will be tortured and killed in El Salvador. As they are driven away, Boyle knows that he will never see them again.

MAJOR MAX

Major Max, the fanatical leader of the Arena Party, speaks to his loyal men at his villa. He calls for death to all Christian Democrats beginning with Archbishop Romero and selects an assassin.

. . . this dumb shit Duarte now has to go back and lick his puta's pussy, the shit-faced faggot every day looks more and more like a watermelon—Christian Democrat green on the outside and when my machete splits him open, Moscow red on the inside! . . . Yes, the time's come now for us brothers—former members of Orden, Patriots of the Maxililio Hernandez Brigade, brothers of the Mano Blanco— (*each sub unit reacting with pride*)—and these fucking priests that are poisoning the minds of our Salvadoran youth are gonna be the first to bleed . . . they're pig shit and this Romero is the biggest pig shit of all—a shit . . . and with this bullet he will be the first to die . . . For every one of our people, we will kill one hundred of them. We will avenge the killers of the South African Ambassador, of Colonel Rosario, of Molina, and Gutierrez and the Mayor of El Paraiso . . . all these shit-faced subversaries that have sold our country out to the Communists will die . . . Duarte, Kelly, Erlich, Zaun, the psuedo-journalists sent here by the Zionist Communist Conspiracy, they will *all* die . . . Now who will be the one among you to rid me of this Romero? Good . . . you . . . (*picks one*) You will be famous. Songs will be sung about you.

ARCHBISHOP ROMERO

In a stirring speech, Archbishop Romero addresses peasants in the cathedral. He calls for an end to the violence and the repression.

The governing junta has good intentions with their promises of land reform and their desire to control the so-called paramilitary forces in the Army, but sadly it is a failure because the power within the junta is the Army, and the Army itself is an obstacle to the reign of God . . . they know only how to repress the people and defend the interests of the rich oligarchy . . . I have called upon the United States, repeatedly, to stop all military aide to this Army unit until it satisfactorily resolves the problems of the disappeared and submits itself to civilian control. Again and again, American aid instead of promoting greater justice and peace is used against the people's organizations fighting to defend their most fundamental human rights—land, education, health, food, shelter. We are poor. You in Washington are so rich. Why are you so blind? My children, you must look to yourselves in this sad time for Salvador. Christians are not afraid of combat; they know how to fight, but they prefer the language of peace. However, when a dictatorship seriously violates human rights and attacks the common good of the nation, when it becomes unbearable and closes all channels of dialogue, when this happens, the Church speaks of the legitimate right of insurrectional violence. The spirit of God has led me to this . . . I would like to close with an appeal to the men of the Army and in particular the National Guard. Brothers, you are part of our people. Yet you kill your own peasant brothers and sisters. But before a man may kill, the law of God must prevail and that law says "Thou Shalt Not Kill!" No soldier is obliged to obey an order against the law of God. Violence on all sides is wrong. Violence is wrong. In the name of God, and in the name of the suffering people whose laments rise to heaven each day more tumultuous, I beg you, I ask you, I order you in the name of God: Stop the repression!

BROADCAST NEWS

1987

20th Century-Fox
Written, Directed, and Produced by James L. Brooks

1 MONOLOGUE
Aaron

SETTING: Washington, D.C., 1980s

Jane is a brilliant young news producer determined to fight the glamour-driven sensationalism of network news. Aaron, a talented correspondent, shares Jane's ideals and dreams about one day becoming the network's anchor. Together they enjoy a bond that makes them an unbeatable broadcast team until handsome Tom Grunick strides into their world.

Although Tom embodies everything that Jane despises about network news—he was hired by the network for his looks, understands next to nothing about the news he reads, and selects stories for their sensational elements—she finds herself becoming hopelessly attracted to him. Aaron is shocked by Jane's interest in Tom and finally confesses his own love for her. Jane can't help her feelings for Tom, however, and the two seem poised on the brink of a love affair.

Aaron quits the network to take a job at a small station in Oregon. Before he leaves, he tells Jane to look at a tape of an interview that Tom had conducted with a rape victim. On the unedited tape Jane sees that Tom stopped the shooting in order to work up some tears for the camera. Enraged by such a callous action, Jane confronts Tom, who shrugs it off. Consequently, she breaks with Tom, who is being sent by the network to London.

Years later, Tom, Jane, and Aaron meet once again in Washington. Tom has just been assigned network anchor, Jane has agreed to be his producer, and Aaron is still in Oregon—now with a wife and family. Their love of the news their only common ground, the three old comrades huddle in a gazebo during a rain shower and talk—not about the past—but about the future.

AARON

In a touching moment, Aaron reveals his feelings for Jane.

You know, I've been doing some of the most important thinking of my life today. I wonder if this is the right time to tell you about it . . . I figured out why I'm so hung up on getting a chance at weekend anchor. It's because if I do it well then they'll pay me more, and my life will be great and they'll treat me better—that's why . . . which means I'm at their mercy—and who wants that? Now, I don't want to tell you where this thought has led me . . . why not? In the middle of all of this, I started to think about the one thing that makes me feel really good and makes immediate sense and it's you . . . I'm going to stop right now except I would give anything if you were two people, so I could call up the one who's my friend and tell her about the one that I like so much. All right, I'm not going to say any more—primarily because I'm about to pass out. Come on, I'll walk you to the corner.

FATAL ATTRACTION

1987

Paramount
A Jaffe Lansing Production
Screenplay by James Dearden
Based on his original screenplay
Directed by Adrian Lyne
Produced by Stanley R. Jaffe and Sherry Lansing

1 MONOLOGUE
Dan

SETTING: New York City, 1980s

Dan Gallagher is a successful attorney who has it all: a beautiful wife, precious daughter, lovely home, good friends—until he meets Alex, a sexy psychopath who turns his life into a living hell.

Dan takes Alex out to supper after a business meeting. His wife Ann and their daughter are spending the weekend in the country, and he finds himself attracted to the overtly seductive Alex. After an intense night of sex, Dan prepares to return home, satisfied with his one night stand. To prevent him from leaving, Alex slashes her wrists, and this is only the beginning.

Alex insanely pursues Dan until he is forced to reveal his affair to Ann, who reacts with hurt and outrage. By this point, Alex has tried to blackmail Dan with claims of pregnancy and has kidnapped his child for a day. She finally sneaks into his house with the intent of killing Ann. The three struggle, and Ann manages to shoot Alex, thus ending Alex's psychotic pursuit of the man she believes destroyed her.

DAN

Alex makes Dan supper in her apartment after their first sexual encounter. As they listen to Madame Butterfly, *Dan tells Alex of the time his father brought him to see that opera at the old Met.*

This is great. I love *Madame Butterfly* . . . it's the first opera I ever saw. My father, he took me to the old Met. I was five years old . . . I got most of it. There was this U.S. sailor setting up house with this Japanese lady. That was all fine, but in the final act, after he left her, my father told me, "She's going to kill herself," and I was terrified, I was . . . I climbed right underneath the chair. It's right here. This is it. It's funny . . . that's one of the only times I remember my father being nice to me when I was a kid: comforting me at *Madame Butterfly.*

FERRIS BUELLER'S DAY OFF

1987

Paramount
Screenplay by John Hughes
Directed by John Hughes
Produced by John Hughes and Tom Jacobson

1 MONOLOGUE
Ferris Bueller

SETTING: Suburban Chicago, 1980s

Ferris Bueller, an inventive and surprisingly philosophical high school senior, is determined to enjoy life as much as possible. Everyone knows and loves Ferris, much to the chagrin of his not-so-adoring younger sister and the high school principal, who appear to be the only two people in their town aware of Ferris's capacity for pranks. On a beautiful spring day, Ferris decides to skip school, taking two friends along for the ride. They drive into Chicago and enjoy many minor adventures and misadventures which add up to the perfect day off.

FERRIS BUELLER

Ferris addresses the audience in the following monologue after having successfully convinced his parents that he is sick and should stay home from school.

They bought it. Incredible. One of the worst performances of my career and they never doubted it for a second. How could I possibly be expected to handle school on a day like today? This is my ninth sick day this semester. It's getting pretty tough coming up with new illnesses. If I go for ten I'm probably going to have to barf up a lung. So I better make this one count. The key to faking-out the parents is clammy hands. It's a good nonspecific symptom. I'm a big believer in it. A lot of people will tell you that a phony fever is a dead lock, but you get a nervous mother and you could wind up in a doctor's office. That's worse than school. You fake a stomach cramp, and when you're bent over, moaning and wailing, you lick your palms. It's a little childish and stupid, but then so is high school. Life moves pretty fast. If you don't stop and look around once in a while you could miss it. I do have a test today. It's on European Socialism. I mean, really, what's the point? I'm not European. I don't plan on being European. So who gives a crap if they're socialists? They could be fascists, it still wouldn't change the fact that I don't own a car. It's not that I condone fascism, or any "ism" for that matter. "Ism's" in my opinion are not good. A person should not believe in an "ism"—he should believe in himself. I quote John Lennon: "I don't believe in Beatles, I just believe in me." A good point there. After all, he was the walrus. I could be the walrus, I'd still have to bum rides off of people.

FULL METAL JACKET

1987

Warner Brothers
Screenplay by Stanley Kubrick, Michael Herr, and
Gustav Hasford
Based on the novel The Short Timers *by Gustav Hasford*
Directed and Produced by Stanley Kubrick

2 MONOLOGUES
Sgt. Hartman
Crazy Earl

SETTING: Parris Island Marine Base and Vietnam, 1968

Full Metal Jacket tells the story of young American men at war. Private Joker is a young man who has joined the Marines to learn how to kill. The film follows Joker's progress from Parris Island to the jungles of Vietnam. At Parris Island, Joker meets Sgt. Hartman: a weathered warrior whose mission is to transform the callow youths into killing machines. This he accomplishes by a twenty-four-hour-a-day barrage of abuse and humiliation—most of which is aimed at Private Pyle, a slow-witted recruit who manages to constantly bring the wrath of Hartman down upon his head. On the last day of basic training, Joker watches in horror as Pyle shoots Hartman and then himself.

We then find Joker in Vietnam on the eve of the Tet Offensive. He is traveling with a platoon commanded by his old friend, Cowboy. When Cowboy is shot by a sniper during the offensive, the enraged platoon storms the burned-out building where the sniper is hiding, only to discover that their leader's killer is a young girl. Fatally wounded by one of the soldiers, the girl begs Joker to kill her. The young man who so badly wanted to be a killer now finds it difficult to actually take a life. Even so, Joker shoots the sniper. The film ends with the ragged platoon marching off into the darkness and singing the Mickey Mouse Club song.

SGT. HARTMAN

Sgt. Hartman greets the new recruits as only he can.

I am Gunnery Sergeant Hartman, your Senior Drill Instructor. From now on, you will speak only when spoken to, and the first and last words out of your filthy sewers will be "Sir!" Do you maggots understand that? Bullshit! I can't hear you. Sound off like you got a pair. If you ladies leave my island, if you survive recruit training . . . you will be a minister of death, praying for war. But until that day you are pukes! You're the lowest form of life on earth. You are not even human fucking beings! You are nothing but unorganized grabasstic pieces of amphibian shit! Because I am hard, you will not like me. But the more you hate me, the more you will learn. I am hard, but I am fair! There is no racial bigotry here! I do not look down on niggers, kikes, wops, or greasers. Here you are all equally worthless! And my orders are to weed out all the non-hackers who do not pack the gear to serve in my beloved Corps! Do you maggots understand that? Bullshit! I can't hear you!

CRAZY EARL

Crazy Earl, a black soldier in Cowboy's platoon, sits next to a dead N.V.A. soldier and introduces him to Joker while extoling the pleasures of killing.

Hey . . . photographer! You want to take a good picture? Here, man . . . take this. This . . . is my bro. This is his party. He's the guest of honor. Today . . . is his birthday. I will never forget this day. The day I came to Hue City and fought one million N.V.A. gooks. I love the little Commie bastards, man. I really do. These enemy grunts are as hard as slant-eyed drill instructors. These are great days we're living, bros! We are jolly green giants, walking the earth with guns. These people we wasted here today . . . are the finest human beings we will ever know. After we rotate back to the world, we're gonna miss not having anyone around that's worth shooting.

MOONSTRUCK

1987

MGM/UA
Screenplay by John Patrick Shanley
Directed by Norman Jewison
Produced by Patrick Palmer and Norman Jewison

2 MONOLOGUES
Ronny
Loretta

SETTING: Brooklyn, 1980s

Loretta Castorini is a thirty-seven-year-old widow who blames her empty life on a run of bad luck. When Johnny Cammareri, an older "mama's boy" proposes, Loretta accepts, thinking that if she follows proper procedure, her luck will change for the better. Loretta's father, Cosmo, is a wealthy plumber who lords over the Castorini family in their Brooklyn brownstone. Cosmo doesn't like Johnny Cammareri, but reluctantly gives his blessing to the upcoming nuptials.

When Johnny receives news that his mother is on her deathbed in Palermo, he flies to Italy to be with her. Before he leaves, he asks Loretta to find his brother, Ronny, with whom he hasn't spoken in many years. Johnny wants to reconcile with his brother and directs Loretta to invite Ronny to their wedding.

When Loretta finds the hot-blooded Ronny, she falls instantly in love with this volatile and handsome young man whose only passion, after losing his hand in a freak accident, is opera.

After a night of lovemaking, Loretta returns home, where she decides to meet with Ronny one more time. They meet at the opera, and Loretta is swept away by the emotional power of *La Boheme*. Ronny convinces her that love is all important, and the following morning a day of truth commences for the Castorini and Cammareri families as all parties converge in the Castorini kitchen.

RONNY

When Loretta goes to Ronny's bakery to ask him to the wedding, he erupts in a rage that is directed at his brother, whom he blames for the loss of his hand.

I have no life. My brother took my life from me and now he's getting married. He has his. He's getting his, and he wants me to come. What is life? They say bread is life, and I bake bread, bread, bread; and shovel this stinking dough in and out of this hot hole in the wall—and I should be so happy. Huh, sweetie? You want me to come to the wedding? Where's my wedding? Chrissy! Over by the wall, bring me the big knife, I'm going to cut my throat. I want you to see this. I want you to watch me kill myself so you can tell my brother, Johnny, on his wedding day, okay? Chrissy, bring me the big knife! She won't do it. Do you know about me? Okay, nothing is anybody's fault, but things happen. Look. This wood, this fake. Five years ago I was engaged to be married, and Johnny came in here and he ordered bread from me and I said, "Oh, okay, some bread," and I put my hand in the slicer and it got caught because I wasn't paying attention. The slicer chewed off my hand. It's funny, 'cause when my fiancée found out about it; when she found out that I had been maimed, she left me for another man. I ain't no freaking monument to justice! I lost my hand! I lost my bride! Johnny has his hand! Johnny has his bride! You want me to take my heartbreak, put it away and forget? Is it just a matter of time before a man opens his eyes and gives up his one dream . . . his one dream of happiness? Maybe . . . maybe.

LORETTA

*Loretta follows Ronny to his apartment immediately following their first
meeting in the bakery. She is obviously captivated by his intensity. She
proceeds to cook him a steak and tries to calm him down by telling him
about her first marriage and suggesting that he isn't the only person to
ever suffer a broken heart.*

What's the matter with you? I mean, you think you're the only one
to ever shed a tear? You got any whiskey? How about you give me a
glass of whiskey? You really are stupid, you know that? Look, I was
raised that a girl gets married young. I held out for love. I got married
when I was twenty-eight. I met a man. I loved him. I married him.
And then he wanted to have a baby right away and I said no, that
we should wait. And then he gets hit by a bus. So, what do I got? I
got no man, no baby, no nothing. You know, how did I know that
this man was a gift—I couldn't keep my one chance of happiness?
You tell me the story, and you act like you know what it means, but
I can see what the true story is and you can't. That woman didn't
leave you, okay? You can't see what you are and I see everything.
You're a wolf. The big part of you has no words and it's a wolf. You
know, that woman was a trap for you—she caught you and you
couldn't get away, so you chewed off your own foot. That was the
price you had to pay for your freedom. You know Johnny had nothing to do with it. You did what you had to do—between you and
you. And now, now you're afraid because you know the big part of
you is a wolf that has the courage to bite off its own hand to save
itself from the trap of the wrong love. That's why there's been no
woman since that wrong woman. Okay? You're scared to death of
what the wolf will do if you try to make that mistake again. I'm
telling you your life.

NADINE

1987

Tri Star
Written and Directed by Robert Benton
Produced by Arlene Donovan

1 MONOLOGUE
Renee

SETTING: Austin, Texas, 1954

This charming comedy tells the story of plucky Nadine Hightower, recently separated from her saloon-owner husband, Vernon. Nadine agrees to pose in several "art studies" for the local photographer, who has assured her that he is best friends with Hugh Hefner. When she discovers that she is pregnant, she tries to get the photos back, and winds up embroiled in a murder and a highway scam.

Nadine cons Vernon into helping her steal back the photos. When he discovers stolen plans hidden inside the envelope, he realizes that the location of the new highway could save his failing bar, the Blue Bonnet.

It becomes clear that Nadine and Vernon are still very much in love as they run from the dangerous Mr. Pope, who orchestrated stealing the plans in the first place. Further complicating matters is Renee, Vernon's daffy girlfriend, whose jealous outbursts place Vernon right into Pope's hands. When Pope has finally been dealt with and Vernon and Nadine are taken into police custody, the sheriff confiscates the stolen plans only to find the "art studies" of Nadine.

As the story ends, Vernon tells Nadine that "Nadine Hightower's World Famous Blue Bonnet Bar" will be the biggest thing to ever hit Texas. Nadine agrees, as long as her name appears in pink neon.

RENEE

Renee confronts Vernon at the Blue Bonnet. She is furious because she found Nadine's negligee at Vernon's place and assumed it was a gift. When she tried to exchange it for the proper size, she was informed that it was used. Vernon's cousin Dwight watches in amusement as Renee lambasts Vernon.

Vernon Hightower, I'm so mad at you, I could bust! Do you see this? This is a size six. I wear a size eight. You would think somebody that's supposed to be my fiancé would know a thing like that. But I'm such a trusting person. I thought it was an honest mistake. So what do I do? I go down to the store and try to exchange it. And what do they tell me? They tell me they cannot take it back because it is a used garment. Used. Futhermore, they haven't had this particular style in the store in six months. Well, I didn't even know Vernon Hightower six months ago! And you're trying to scare me with that thing won't work. You must have told me a dozen times already about how you keep that gun in the ice chest just for show— 'bout how the firing pin is jammed and it won't shoot. Here! As far as I'm concerned, we are no longer engaged.

ORPHANS

1987

Lorimar Motion Pictures
Screenplay by Lyle Kessler
Based on his play
Directed by Alan J. Pakula
Produced by Alan J. Pakula

1 MONOLOGUE
Harold

SETTING: Newark, New Jersey, 1980s

Treat and Philip are brothers who have been abandoned by their parents. They live in an old two-story home which is the only house left standing in a ruined neighborhood of Newark. Treat is street smart and violent, but is possessed of a misplaced sense of morality which he never fails to express.

Philip, on the other hand, is asthmatic and sickly. Treat has convinced him that the outside air will kill him, so he never leaves the house. Treat takes his guardianship of Philip very seriously, and thwarts any effort made by his brother to do things for himself.

One night, Treat brings home Harold, a man he's followed to a bar with the intent of stealing his briefcase. Harold buys him some drinks, and Treat cons the drunken Harold into coming home with him.

Harold, it turns out, is a very serious gangster; more than a match for the impetuous Treat. An orphan himself, however, he feels an affinity with the brothers.

Harold draws Philip out of his shell and shows him that he can leave the house. He gives Philip a map, so he'll never get lost, and instills confidence in the young man who had been trapped for so long.

Treat is filled with rage when he realizes that Harold has liberated Philip and the film ends in a dramatic confrontation between the two brothers.

HAROLD

Drunk and close to passing out, Harold tells Treat and Philip about the orphanage he grew up in.

I come from an orphanage; a god damn orphanage. No "top o' the mornin' " Irish mother there, either. Just a big, son-of-a-bitching German. He wore a chef's hat and a dirty filthy apron and he slept right in the kitchen. Orphans are always hungry. Orphans love to creep down in the middle of the night and raid the refrigerator. But the German slept right there, one eye open. He'd break every bone in your back if he caught you. He'd break every bone in your body. He took a liking to me, though. He used to fill my plate with meat and potatoes. Was lucky for me. Orphans always coughing up blood. Orphans dropping dead all the time. There's a terrible mortality rate in an orphange. Thank God for them big heaping plates of meat and potatoes. Thank God for that big fucking German son-of-a-bitch. You know what orphans call out in the middle of the night, Treat? Motherless orphans in the middle of this night? Chicago orphans on a big hill facing Lake Michigan? The wind used to come through there and make a terrible sound. The wind used to come through there and go, Whooo-ooooo! Frightened orphans pulling their blankets up over their heads. Frightened orphans crying out. You know what they're crying? "Mommy!" Honest to God. "Mommy." Orphans don't know the difference between a mommy and a daddy. They don't know the difference between a mommy and a fucking tangerine. The poor motherless bastards.

SALOME'S LAST DANCE

A KEN RUSSELL FILM OF AN OSCAR WILDE STORY

1987

Vestron Pictures
Screenplay by Ken Russell
Incorporating Oscar Wilde's play,
Salome, *translated from the french by Vivian Russell.*
Directed by Ken Russell
Produced by Penny Corke

1 MONOLOGUE
Salome

SETTING: A brothel in Victorian London

This eerie and erotic film tells a story of Oscar Wilde, the irrepressibly decadent British playwright. When his scandalous version of *Salome* was banned by Parliament, Wilde's good friend—the middle-aged proprieter of one of London's imfamous bordellos—arrange to produce the play in the brothel for Oscar's amusement.

Herod, Herodius, Salome, and John the Baptist are all portrayed by the regular denizens of this den of iniquity. Wilde is delighted as his play comes to life before his eyes. The brothel master himself plays the cowardly Herod, a man haunted by the stinging words of the prophet whom he keeps imprisoned at his court.

The brothel's meek little chamber maid is utterly transformed by playing the seductive Salome, the spoiled princess of Judea who brought about the death of John the Baptist. Wilde's lover plays the doomed prophet. He brings dark passion to the part as he jealously watches Wilde cavort with a young boy in the audience. The film offers a dream-like vision of Wilde's life and play that sometimes borders on nightmare.

SALOME

*The spoiled princess dances for Herod, her lascivious stepfather, and in
return, he agrees to execute John the Baptist and deliver the prophet's head
to the princess on a silver platter. Alone with the prophet's head, Salome
pours out her rage and unrequited love for the dead man who so scornfully
rejected her in life.*

There isn't any noise. I can hear nothing. Why doesn't he cry out?
If someone was trying to kill me I'd scream and fight. I wouldn't
want to suffer. Strike! Strike, I tell you! I hear nothing. Ahh, you
didn't want to let me kiss you, John the Baptist. Well, I will kiss
you now. I will bite your mouth with my teeth the way I bite into a
ripe fruit. Yes, I'll bite your mouth, John the Baptist. I told you so,
didn't I? I told you. Well, I will kiss it now. But, why don't you look
at me, John the Baptist? Your eyes, which were so terrible, so full of
anger and contempt, are closed now. And your tongue that was like
a red snake darting poison, it doesn't move anymore, it doesn't say
anything now, John the Baptist. That red viper who vomited his
venom on me—strange, isn't it? Why is it that the red snake is still?
You didn't want me, you rejected me. You said infamous things to
me. You treated me like a courtesan, a whore. Me, Salome, daughter
of Herodius, Princess of Judea! So now, John the Baptist, I am still
alive, but you are dead. And your head is mine. I can do with it as
I please. I can throw it to the dogs or the birds of the air. What the
dogs leave the birds will eat. John the Baptist, John the Baptist; you
were the only man I ever loved. All the others filled me with disgust.
But you, you were beautiful. Your body was an ivory column on a
silver pedestal. It was a garden filled with doves and silver lillies. It
was a silver tower adorned with ivory shields. There was nothing in
the world as white as your body. There was nothing in the world as
black as your hair. In all the world, there was nothing as red as your
mouth. Your voice was a censer filled with strange perfumes. And
when I looked at you, I heard strange music. Oh, why didn't you
look at me, John the Baptist? You hid your face behind your hands
and your blasphemy. You placed on your eyes the bandage of one

who wishes to see his god, well, you have seen him; your god. But me, me! You have never seen me. Oh, how I loved you. I love you still, John the Baptist. I love only you. I am thirsty for your beauty. I am hungry for your body, and neither wine nor fruit can appease my desire. Tell me what to do now, John the Baptist. Neither rivers nor floods can drown my passion. I was a princess and you humiliated me. I was a virgin and you raped me. I was chaste and you filled my veins with fire. Why didn't you look at me, John the Baptist? If you had looked at me you would have loved me. I know you would have loved me. And the mystery of love is greater than the mystery of death. One must only look to love.

THE WHALES OF AUGUST

1987

Alive Films, Inc. and Nelson Entertainment
With Circle Associates, LTD
Screenplay by David Berry
Based upon his play
Directed by Lindsay Anderson
Produced by Carolyn Pfeiffer and Mike Kaplan

1 MONOLOGUE
Sarah

SETTING: An island off the coast of Maine, 1980s

Libby and Sarah are two widowed sisters facing the inevitability of old age and death. The sisters live together in an old house on a cliff above the sea. Libby has lost her sight and relies on Sarah for everything. Spunky Sarah bustles around the house and grounds, annoying Libby with her ceaseless energy.

Libby is obsessed with death to the point that she no longer considers herself to be one of the living. When Sarah expresses a desire to put in a picture window, Libby scornfully reminds her that they are too old to enjoy a view of the sea.

Sarah doesn't know what to do with Libby, who becomes more of a burden every day. On the eve of her forty-sixth wedding anniversary, she confronts Libby with her concerns for their futures. As Libby has embraced death, Sarah has embraced life—and there is no compromise.

That night, Sarah toasts her husband, Phillip, who was killed in WW I. Her passion for living and indomitable spirit are echoed in the memories she recounts for Phillip's photograph.

Libby finally realizes that life does in fact go on, and tells Sarah that she should get the picture window. The film ends with the two women walking down to the bluff from which they used to watch whales when they were girls. Sarah bemoans the fact that the whales don't come anymore and Libby hopefully suggests that they just might show, for life has a way of fooling us, and usually does.

SARAH

On her forty-sixth wedding anniversary, Sarah dresses in a blue chiffon gown and toasts the photograph of her husband with red wine. She thinks back over the years to when they were first in love and shares a cherished memory of that time in their lives together.

Forty-six years, Phillip. Forty-six red roses; forty-six white. White for truth—red for passion. That's what you always said: "Passion and truth; that's all we need." I wish you were here, Phillip. I don't know what to do about Libby. She seems to have become so bitter. She was so cruel about Mr. Maranov and she won't have our picture window. She says we're too old—our lives are over. I don't think I can manage her much longer. Oh, if only you were here, Phillip. Oh, Phillip, my corset has so many stays and so many ties. You said, "Too many, my love. The moon will set before I have you completely undone." But I said, "Never, my love. I won't be entirely undone—even by you. For what mystery would keep you with me if you unwrap them all?"

THE WITCHES OF EASTWICK

1987

Warner Brothers
Screenplay by Michael Cristofer
Based on the novel by John Updike
Directed by George Miller
Produced by Neil Canton, Peter Guber, and Jon Peters

3 MONOLOGUES
Darryl Van Horn 1
Alex
Darryl Van Horn 2

SETTING: Eastwick, Rhode Island, 1980s

Three beautiful women—who just happen to be witches—gather for their weekly evening of martinis and gossip. Their conversation inevitably turns to men, and each reveals their own requirements for a "perfect man." Enter Darryl Van Horn, a handsome devil who is more than happy to answer the witches' unwitting summons. His arrival in the sleepy little town of Eastwick—which bears a striking resemblance to Salem, Massachusetts—heralds wicked fun, diabolic lust, and eventual disaster for the three witches, who discover that perfection in a man is a highly overrated commodity.

DARRYL VAN HORN 1

Darryl Van Horn attempts to seduce Alex, the artistic witch whose husband has recently died. His powers of persuasion are top notch, as seen in this most compelling speech. Lonely Alex easily falls under the devil's spell.

Fidel, that's his name. Women love him. They're crazy about him. He has a big schlong. Huge. Well, there you are; scale again, size. I don't know, maybe it's a masculine thing. They say women don't care. I'm sort of in the middle myself. How about you? You see, women are in touch with different things. That's my opinion. I know it's not a fashionable opinion right now, but fuck it, I know what I see. I see men running around, trying to put their dicks into everything, trying to make something happen. But it's women who are the source. The only power. Nature. Birth. Rebirth. Cliché, cliché. Sure, but true. I like women. I admire them. But if you want me to treat you like a dumb twit, I will. But what's the point? You have brains, Alex. More than brains, and you don't even know it, do you? Well, most women do not. Where's your husband? When a woman unloads a husband or a husband unloads a woman—however it happens—Death, Desertion, Divorce; the three D's. When that happens, a woman blooms. She blossoms, like flowers, like fruit. She is ripe. That's the woman for me. Would you like to see my house? In case anybody ever needs any exercise, the pool's right over there past the piano where the ballroom used to be. Interesting word: ballroom. And over there is my study. Ah, this is my bedroom. The Borgias once owned the bed. Of course, you have to pay for it with your soul, but what the hell? I deserve a little luxury. You have to take care of yourself. No one's going to do that for you, are they? I'm being as direct with you as I know how. I thought you might appreciate it. Anyway, I always like a little pussy after lunch. What do you say? Hmmm? I would never insult your intelligence with something as trivial as seduction. But I would love to fuck you.

ALEX

Alex rails against Van Horn's attempts to seduce her in this angry speech made moments before she finally surrenders to his otherwordly charms.

Are you trying to seduce me? Well, I have to admit that I appreciate your directness, Darryl, and I will try to be as direct and honest with you as I possibly can be. I think—no, I am positive—that you are the most unattractive man I have ever met in my entire life. You know, in the short time we've been together you have demonstrated every loathsome characteristic of the male personality and even discovered a few new ones. You are physically repulsive, intellectually retarded, you're morally reprehensible, vulgar, insensitive, selfish, stupid, you have no taste, a lousy sense of humor, and you smell. You're not even interesting enough to make me sick. Goodbye, Darryl, and thank you for a lovely lunch.

DARRYL VAN HORN 2

The witches have had enough of Darryl and decide to use his own spells against him in a hilarious sequence that sends the little devil flying— literally—into a packed church on Sunday morning. When presented with such a captive audience on his chief competitor's home turf, he cannot resist making an impromptu speech on the foibles of the fairer sex.

Sorry, just having a little trouble; trouble at home. Little domestic problem. Nothing to be alarmed at, just a little female problem. Ungrateful little bitches, aren't they? May I ask you something? You're all church-going folk. I really want to ask you something. Do you think God knew what he was doing when he created woman? No shit, I really want to know. Or do you think it was another one of his minor mistakes? Like tidal waves, earthquakes, floods! Do you think women are like that? What's the matter? You don't think God makes mistakes? Of course he does! We all make mistakes. Of course, when we make mistakes they call it "evil," when God makes mistakes they call it "nature." So, what do you think? Women: a mistake—or did He do it to us on purpose? Because I really want to know. Because, if it's a mistake, maybe we can do something about it. Find a cure. Invent a vaccine. Build up our immune systems. Get a little exercise. You know, twenty push-ups a day and you never have to be afflicted with women again. Eat broccoli.

BULL DURHAM

1988

Orion Pictures
Screenplay by Ron Shelton
Directed by Ron Shelton
Produced by Thom Mount and Mark Burg

1 MONOLOGUE
Annie Savoy

SETTING: Durham, North Carolina, 1980s

Annie Savoy is a smart sexy lady whose single passion in life is baseball. She follows the Durham Bulls with all the loyalty and dedication of a manager—a function she performs for free, from the stands. Annie selects one player every season on whom to bestow her charms and wisdom. She uses sex, fantasy, and the poetry of Walt Whitman to instill a sense of confidence and grace into the young players she romances.

This year, Annie has her eye on Ebbie Calvin "Nuke" La-Louche, a young pitcher with his head in the clouds and an arm of solid platinum. The savvy Annie easily seduces Ebbie, but a fly appears in her ointment with the appearance of "Crash" Davis, a seasoned catcher sent in to help train Ebbie for the majors. Crash is a passionate man who longs for something meaningful from life—the very thing that Annie has been trying to avoid.

The season progresses, and Nuke, under Annie and Crash's tutelage, learns what it takes to be a winner. At the end of the season he wins his chance to play for the majors. At the same time, Crash loses his contract, but it is then that Crash and Annie find their way to one another, finally ready to settle down and start a new life together.

ANNIE SAVOY

Annie Savoy, the patron saint of Durham baseball players, here speaks of her love for the game, comparing it to the world's great religions.

I believe in the church of baseball. I tried all the major religions and most of the minor ones. I've worshipped Buddha, Allah, Brahma, Vishnu, Siva, trees, mushrooms, and Isadora Duncan. I know things. For instance, there are one hundred eight beads in a catholic rosary and one hundred eight stitches on a baseball. When I learned that, I gave Jesus a chance. But it just didn't work out between us. The Lord lay too much guilt on me. I prefer metaphysics to theology. You see, there's no guilt in baseball, and it's never boring, which makes it like sex. There's never been a ball player who's slept with me who didn't have the best year of his career. Making love is like hitting a baseball. You just got to relax and concentrate. Besides, I'd never sleep with a player hitting under .250 unless he had a lot of RBI's and was a great glove man up the middle. You see, there's a certian amount of life wisdom I give these boys. Sometimes when I've got a ball player alone, I'll just read Emily Dickinson or Walt Whitman to him. And the guys are so sweet, they always stay and listen. Of course, a guy will listen to anything if he thinks it's fore-play. I make them feel confident and they make me feel safe, and pretty. Of course, what I give them lasts a lifetime. What they give me lasts one hundred forty-two games. Sometimes that seems like a bad trade, but bad trades are part of baseball. Who can forget Frank Robinson or Milt Pappas for God's sake? It's a long season, and you gotta trust it. I've tried them all, I really have, and the only church that truly feeds the soul is the church of baseball.

THE LAST TEMPTATION
OF CHRIST

1988

Universal Pictures and Cineplex Odeon Films
Screenplay by Paul Schrader
Based on the book by Nikos Kazantzakis
Directed by Martin Scorsese
Produced by Barbara De Fina

1 MONOLOGUE
Jesus

SETTING: The Holy Land during the time of Christ.

As a carpenter in Nazareth, Jesus is employed by the Romans to make crosses for crucifixions. Mary Magdalen, his childhood love, is now spurned so that he may maintain purity. Judas is an assassin sent by Saul to kill Jesus in the desert.

The story proceeds upon its inevitable course until the moment of the crucifixion when Satan sends his final temptation to Jesus. In an elaborate hallucination, a beautiful young girl leads Jesus to believe that he has been spared the cross. He is led down from the cross by the angel and is allowed to live as a real man. He makes love, fathers children, and grows old. Jesus almost succumbs to this temptation, but realizes at the last moment that he must return to the agony of the cross.

Fewer films have sparked greater debate than this unique and thought-provoking retelling of the New Testament.

JESUS

While visiting a monastery in the desert, Jesus speaks with a monk about God and his own sins.

You think it's a blessing to know what God wants? I'll tell you what he wants. He wants to push me over. Can't he see what's inside of me? All my sins? I'm a liar; a hypocrite. I'm afraid of everything. I don't ever tell the truth—I don't have the courage. When I see a woman, I blush and turn away. I want her, but I don't take her—for God, and that makes me proud, and then my pride wrongs Magdalen. I don't steal, I don't fight, I don't kill—not because I don't want to, but because I'm afraid. I want to rebel against you—against everything—against God. But I'm afraid. You want to know who my mother and father are? You want to know who my god is? Fear. You look inside me and that's all you'll find. Lucifer is inside me. He says to me, "You're not the son of King David. You're not a man. You're the son of man—and more—the son of God, and more than that: God. Do you want to ask me anything else?

TUCKER: THE MAN
AND HIS DREAM

1988

Lucasfilms, Ltd.
Screenplay by Arnold Schulman and David Seider
Directed by Francis Ford Coppola
Produced by Fred Roos and Fred Fuchs

2 MONOLOGUES
Abe
Tucker

SETTING: Chicago, 1945

Preston Tucker was a man with a dream—several, in fact. Inventor and family man, Tucker knew that when the GI's returned home from WWII, the nation's economy would change drastically. He saw the coming of the baby boom and knew that if he could invent a car that would represent the future, he would become a very rich man.

Abe Karatz, a financial shark with a shady background, is convinced by Tucker's presentation that the Tucker Torpedo is such a car, and the two go into business together. In a daring move, Tucker advertises the Torpedo—which hasn't even been made yet—in a national magazine, and letters and orders pour in from all over the country. Abe and Tucker obtain federal funding in Washington and buy a factory in Chicago where production on the Torpedo begins.

Unknown to Tucker and Abe, the "Big Three" auto makers in Detroit have no intention of allowing the Torpedo to be made. They fear that they will have to spend millions to keep up with its superior design and Tucker's low-cost manufacturing. Tucker then finds himself the target of an SEC investigation culminating in an emotional trial in which he is accused of attempting to default on the loan. Tucker addresses the jury directly, and manages to convince them of his innocence, but only fifty models of the amazing Tucker Torpedo exist to bear witness to the dreams and ingenuity of an American original.

ABE

Abe has been informed of the impending investigation. He wants to resign before his past conviction for bank fraud can be used against Tucker. Here he tearfully confronts his friend with the truth of his past.

Okay. I did three years in the pen for bank fraud . . . so they'll use it against you . . . the whole ten years since I been in the pen it never bothered me for two seconds that I'm an ex-con. Why should it? Who cared? But for you and Nora and the kids to know . . . I'm ashamed. When I was a little kid—maybe five years old in the old country, my mother used to say to me—she'd warn me, she'd say to me, "Don't get too close to people, you'll catch their dreams." Years later I realized I misunderstood her. Germs, she said, not dreams, "You'll catch their germs." I want you to know something, Tucker, I went into business with you for one reason: to make money. That's all. How was I to know that if I got too close I'd catch your dreams?

TUCKER

Tucker insists on being allowed to speak in lieu of his attorney, making a closing statement at the end of his trial. Here he manages to sway the jury with his vision of free enterprise.

When I was a boy I used to read all about Edison and the Wright Brothers—Mr. Ford—they were my heroes. Rags to riches: that's not just the name of a book, that's what this country was all about. We invented the free enterprise system where anybody—no matter who he was, where he came from, what class he belonged to—if he came up with a better idea, about anything, there was no limit to how far he could go. I grew up a generation too late, I guess, because now the way the system works the loner, the dreamer, the crackpot who comes up with some crazy idea that everybody laughs at later, turns out to revolutionize the world—he's squashed from above before he even gets his head out of the water because the bureaucrats, they'd rather kill a new idea than let it rock the boat. If Benjamin Franklin were alive today he'd be thrown in jail for sailing a kite without a license! It's true. We're all puffed-up with ourselves now because we invented the Bomb—beat the daylights out of the Japanese, the Nazis—but if big business closes the door on the little guy with the new idea, we're not only closing the door on progress, but we're sabotaging everything that we've fought for. Everything that the country stands for! And one day we're going to find ourselves at the bottom of the heap instead of king of the hill having no idea how we got there: buying our radios and our cars from our former enemies. I don't believe that's going to happen—I can't believe it because if I ever stop believing the plain old common horse sense of the American people, there'd be no way I could get out of bed in the morning. Thank you.

MISSISSIPPI BURNING

1988

Orion
Screenplay by Chris Gerolomo
Directed by Alan Parker
Produced by Frederick Zollo and Robert F. Colesberry

2 MONOLOGUES
Rupert
Mrs. Pell

SETTING: Jessup County, Mississippi, 1964

Rupert Anderson and Alan Ward are FBI agents assigned to investigate the disappearance of three young civil rights activists in Mississippi during the volatile summer of 1964. What they find upon their arrival in Jessup County is a town so filled with hate and rage that an explosion between the races is imminent.

For a while it seems that the FBI and all of its resources are no match for the closely knit southern society that is led by the Ku Klux Klan hate-mongers responsible for the murder of the activists. The young and idealistic Alan Ward believes that strict adherence to Bureau procedure will flush out the guilty parties, whereas the older and more experienced Rupert knows that they will have to resort to more dire methods. Alan finally agrees, and violence is met with violence. The killers are unmasked and the FBI withdraws to let time and understanding heal the rift between black and white.

RUPERT

Rupert, a Mississippian himself, tells Alan a story about his father that he hopes will explain the depth of Southern prejudice.

You know, when I was a little boy, there was an old negro farmer that lived down the road from us name of Monroe. And he was, I guess he was just a little luckier than my daddy was. He bought himself a mule. That was a big deal around that town. Now my daddy hated that mule because his friends were always kidding him about how they saw Monroe out plowing with his new mule, and Monroe was going to rent another field now that he had a mule, and one morning that mule just showed up dead. They poisoned the water. And after that there was never any mention about that mule around my daddy . . . just never came up. 'Til one time we were driving down the road and we passed Monroe's place and we saw it was empty. He just packed up and left, I guess. Gone up north or something. I looked over at my daddy's face and I knew he'd done it and he saw that I knew. He was ashamed. I guess he was ashamed. And he looked at me and he said, "If you ain't better than a nigger, son, then who are you better than?" An old man who was just so full of hate that he didn't know that being poor was what was killing him.

MRS. PELL

One of the chief suspects is Deputy Pell. Rupert senses that Pell's wife is a good woman and will eventually confess what she knows about the matter. Here she breaks down and tells Rupert where the bodies are hidden.

It's not good for you to be here. It's ugly. This whole thing is so ugly. Have you any idea what it's like to live with all this? People look at us and all they see is bigots and racists. Hatred isn't something you're born with. It gets taught. At school they said segregation what's said in the Bible. Genesis nine verse twenty-seven. At seven years of age you get told it enough times you believe it. You believe the hatred. You live it. You breathe it. You marry it. My husband drove one of the cars that night. That's what you want to hear, isn't it? The bodies are buried on the Roberts farm in an earthen dam.

THE ACCUSED

1989

Paramount
Screenplay by Tom Topor
Directed by Jonathan Kaplan
Produced by Stanley R. Jaffe and Sherry Lansing

1 MONOLOGUE
Sarah

SETTING: Oregon, 1980s

Based on an actual event, *The Accused* tells the story of Sarah To-bias, a young woman who is brutally gang-raped in a bar while a large crowd of men watch and cheer the rapists on. When the case comes to trial, Deputy District Attorney Kathryn Murphy accepts plea bargains from the accused's lawyers and the men are sent to jail on lesser charges. Enraged, Sarah finds Kathryn and denounces her for not caring about what really happened. Chastened, Kathryn re-solves to prosecute the men who cheered the rapists on, hoping to establish a legal precedent.

Sarah bravely counters all the claims made against her by the defendants' attorneys throughout the emotional trial. When it is all over, Kathryn has won her case and Sarah has won back her self-esteem. This landmark case was a victory for all women.

SARAH

Sarah is called to testify at the climax of the trial. Here she describes the horror and pain of being raped.

My boyfriend and I had kind of a fight so I got in my car and I drove to see my girlfriend, Sally, at the Mill. I figured she'd be getting off work and we could talk. She's a waitress, just like me. So, anyway— she was on a break. We were sitting in this booth, talking, and this guy, Danny, sent over a couple of drinks. She knew him, so we took the drinks and he sat down and we started talking and he was funny, you know, he had a line. A bunch of the guys went into the back room to play pinball, so me and Danny went in and started playing with this guy, Bob, and after I finished my turn I went to go have a smoke—you know, smoke a little pot—and somebody put some money in the jukebox and this song I really liked came on the jukebox so I started to dance and then Danny comes up and he starts dancing with me, real close, you know, tight close. And he kissed me. I let him kiss me because I figured he was drunk and he was stoned and he would kiss me and then he would leave me alone. And then he put his hand up my shirt and he grabbed at my breasts and I tried to push him away but he kept pulling me closer and he put his hand on my throat. But he's a really strong guy, you know? And the next thing I know he was squeezing my throat with his hands and he pushed me down on the pinball machine and he ripped my shirt. He lifted my skirt. He pulled down my underpants really . . . really hard. I wanted to move, but he was holding me down really hard and he was jamming . . . he was kissing me very hard and he was jamming his hand up my crotch. I heard a bunch of people yelling, "Hold her down! Hold her down!" And then, the big guy, Kurt, held my arms down and I could hear them yelling and clapping and cheering and then . . . then he put his hand over my mouth . . . over my face and I shut my eyes. He was inside of me. And then . . . and then they switched. I could hear them saying, "Frat boy! Frat boy!" and then Bob was inside of me and there was all this yelling and clapping and laughing and then I heard them call for Kurt, "Needle dick! Needle dick!" and they switched again. And Kurt was inside of me. And they were yelling, "Kurt! Kurt! Kurt!" and there was all this chanting . . . something, "Poke that pussy!" Yeah. And I kicked, I kicked really hard and I ran into the road. This guy picked me up and took me to the hospital.

WHEN HARRY MET SALLY

1989

Columbia
Screenplay by Nora Ephron
Directed by Rob Reiner
Produced by Rob Reiner and Andrew Scheinman

2 MONOLOGUES
Harry
Sally

SETTING: New York City, the present

It's irritation-at-first-sight for Harry Burns and Sally Albright when they meet after graduating college in the 1970s. The two are thrown together by circumstance as they share a ride from Chicago to New York and by the time they arrive at Washington Square, it's nothing short of a miracle that they haven't killed one another.

Over the years, Harry and Sally kept bumping into one another, and they finally form a reluctant friendship. Harry finds that he can tell Sally things he can't tell anyone else, and Sally discovers that Harry is warm and funny. They become inseparable buddies, their love for one another apparent to everyone except to them.

One night, they end up in bed together and when Harry tries lamely to extricate himself from responsibility and the possibility of commitment, Sally severs all ties with him. Miserable, Harry walks the streets and finds only emptiness. He realizes, too late, that he loves Sally. On New Year's Eve, he finds her and declares his love. She forgives him and presumably they live happily ever after.

HARRY

Harry tells his friend, Jess, of the callous way that his wife left him.

Friday, Helen comes home from work, and she says, "I don't know if I want to be married anymore." Like it's the institution, you know, like it's nothing personal, just something she's been thinking about in a casual way. I'm calm. I say, "Why don't we take some time to think about it?" You know, don't rush into anything. Next day, she says she's thought about it, and she wants a trial separation. She just wants to try it, she says. But we can still date, she says, like this is supposed to cushion the blow. I mean, I got married so I could stop dating, so I don't see where "we can still date" is a big incentive, since the last thing you want to do is date your wife, who's supposed to love you, which is what I'm saying to her when it occurs to me that maybe she doesn't, so I say to her, "Don't you love me anymore?" and you know what she says? "I don't know if I've ever loved you." Then she tells me that someone in her office is going to South America, and she can sublet his apartment. I can't believe this. And the doorbell rings. "I can sublet his apartment." The words are still hanging in the air, you know, like a balloon connected to her mouth. So I'm going to the door, and there are moving men there. Now I start to get suspicious. I say, "Helen, when did you call the movers?" And she doesn't say anything, so I ask the movers, "When did this woman book you for this gig?" and they're just standing there, three huge guys, one of them wearing a T-shirt that says, "Don't fuck with Mister Zero." So I said, "Helen, when did you make this arrangement?" She says, "A week ago." I said, "You've known for a week, and you didn't tell me?" And she says, "I didn't want to ruin your birthday."

SALLY

Sally tells Harry about her relationship with Joe and her decision to break it off with him.

When Joe and I started seeing each other, we wanted exactly the same thing. We wanted to live together, but we didn't want to get married because every time anyone we knew got married, it ruined their relationship. They practically never had sex again. It's true, it's one of the secrets no one ever tells you. I would sit around with my girlfriends who have kids—well, actually, my one girlfriend who has kids, Alice—and she would complain about how she and Gary never did it anymore. She didn't even complain about it, now that I think about it. She just said it matter-of-factly. She said they were up all night, they were both exhausted all the time, the kids just took every sexual impulse they had out of them. And Joe and I used to talk about it, and we'd say we were so lucky to have this wonderful relationship, we can have sex on the kitchen floor and not worry about the kids walking in, we can fly off to Rome on a moment's notice. And then one day I was taking Alice's little girl for the afternoon because I'd promised to take her to the circus, and we were in a cab playing "I Spy"—I spy a mailbox, I spy a lamppost—and she looked out the window and she saw this man and this woman with these two little kids, the man had one of the kids on his shoulders, and Alice's little girl said, "I spy a family," and I started to cry. You know, I just started crying. And I went home, and I said, "The thing is, Joe, we never do fly off to Rome on a moment's notice."

sex, lies, and videotape

1989

RCA/Columbia
Written and Directed by Steven Soderbergh

2 MONOLOGUES
Graham
Ann

SETTING: Baton Rouge, Louisiana, the present

Graham Dalton is a twenty-nine-year-old drifter who travels the country in search of himself. The impotent Graham can only become aroused by viewing videotaped confessions of strange women whom he has encountered along his journey.

In Baton Rouge, Graham calls on John Millany, a friend from college. John is married to the beautiful Ann and having an affair with her sister, Cynthia.

The repressed Ann is as fascinated by Graham as he is by her, and they eventually awaken one another's sexualities. With Graham's help, Ann is finally able to admit the failure of her marriage. She leaves John and forgives her sister. She and Graham then embark upon a life together that is full of promise and hope.

GRAHAM

When Graham first appears at her house, Ann is quite fascinated with his nonconventional views on life. She marvels at how different he is from John. When she tells Graham that she feels as though her marriage is speeding by, he responds with some unusual metaphysics.

Did you know that if you shut someone up in a room, and the only clock he has reference to runs two hours slow for every twenty-four, that his body will eventually adjust to that schedule? Simply because the mind honestly perceives that twenty-six hours are twenty-four, the body follows. And then there are sections of time. Your life can be broken down into the sections of time that formed your personality (if you have one). For instance, when I was twelve, I had an eleven minute conversation with my father that to this day defines our relationship. Now, I'm not saying that everything happened in that specific section of time, but the events of my childhood involving my father led up to, and then were crystallized in, that eleven minutes. Anyway, I think the mind is very flexible as far as time is concerned. Exactly. I would say the fact that you feel the first year of your marriage has gone by quickly means lots of things. Or *could* mean lots of things.

ANN

Ann has just discovered that her husband and sister are sleeping together. She goes to Graham and vents her rage. She is aware of his tape collection, and now wants to make her own "confession."

My life is . . . shit. It's all shit. It's like somebody saying, "Okay, chairs are not chairs, they're actually swimming pools." I mean, nothing is what I thought it was. What happened to me? Have I been asleep? I vaguely remember the wedding, but a lot of it is just a blur . . . like I was watching from a distance. I can't *believe* him. Why didn't I trust my intuition? And I'm vacuuming his goddamn rug. *His* rug, that *he* paid to have put in *his* house. Nothing in that place belongs to me. I wanted to put some of my grandmother's furniture in it, but he wouldn't let me. So I'm vacuuming *his* rug. That bastard. I want to make a tape.

APPENDIX:
MONOLOGUES BY GENDER
AND AGE

HOW TO USE THIS CHART

The following chart has been created to help you with your search for the perfect monologue. Simply turn to the appropriate sex (i.e., male or female!) and scan the columns. You will see that we have broken the monologues down by age range and type. If you're an eighteen-year-old male looking for a comedic piece, you can easily see that *Ferris Bueller's Day Off* may have what you're looking for. The age ranges presented here are merely suggestive of the roles as they have been written and are not meant to restrict the imagination of the actor, but please note that most directors prefer that actors select monologues that closely reflect both their age and the role they are auditioning for. Good luck!

GENRE CODES
D = Dramatic
C = Comic
SC = Serio-Comic

Film	Setting

MEN

River's Edge	Oregon, 1980s
Ferris Bueller's Day Off	Suburban Chicago, 1980s
Platoon	Vietnam, 1967
The Sure Thing	A New England college, the present
Harold and Maude	The American Southwest, early 1970s
Creator	An American university, the present
Birdy	An Army mental hospital, during the Vietnam conflict

Character	Genre	Age	Page
John A disturbed young man who has murdered his girlfriend. (2 monologues)	D	16–18	89
Ferris A cocky yet philosophical high school senior.	C	18	98
Chris A newly arrived G.I. (2 monologues)	D	18-20	85
Gib A carefree college student attracted to a beautiful but straight-laced classmate.	D	18-20	74
Harold A young man obsessed with death.	SC	Early 20s	28
Boris A passionate young man fighting to save his girlfriend's life.	D	Early 20s	66
Al An injured vet fighting to save his best friend from insanity.	D	20s	62

Film	Setting
sex, lies, and videotape	Baton Rouge, La., the present
Platoon	Vietnam, 1967
Full Metal Jacket	Vietnam, 1968
Taxi Driver	NYC, the present
Blade Runner	Los Angeles, 2019
When Harry Met Sally	NYC, the present
The Last Temptation of Christ	The desert
Moonstruck	Brooklyn, 1980s

Character	Genre	Age	Page
Graham A romantic, but impotent, young man.	D	20s	133
Rhah A seasoned soldier with a taste for marijuana.	D	20-30	86
Crazy Earl A battle-weary black GI.	D	20-30	101
Travis A psychotic living on the edge.	D	20-30	32
Roy Blatty A renegade android fighting to stay "alive."	D	30s	39
Harry A man whose wife has just left him.	SC	30s	131
Jesus The son of God expresses anger about his fate.	D	30s	121
Ronny A man made bitter by the loss of his hand and his pride.	SC	30s	104

Film	Setting
Coming Home	California, 1960s
Platoon	Vietnam, 1967
The Days of Wine and Roses	San Francisco, 1960s
The Agony and the Ecstasy	16th-century Rome
. . . And Justice For All	The United States, 1970s
Nate and Hayes	South Pacific, mid-1800s
Repo Man	Los Angeles, 1980s
Repo Man	Los Angeles, 1980s

Character	Genre	Age	Page
Luke A disabled Vietnam vet.	SC	30s	34
Elias A philosophical Army sergeant.	D	30s	87
Joe Clay A successful PR man driven to the edge of sanity by alcholism.	D	30-40	11
Michelangelo A man driven by passion for his art.	D	30-40	22
Arthur Kirkland A disenchanted attorney trying to fight the system.	SC	30-40	36
"Bully" Hayes A pirate with a heart of gold.	SC	30-40	44
Repo Man A man devoted to his work.	SC	30-40	46
Miller The repossession company's mechanic; a philosophical oddball.	SC	30-40	46

Film	Setting
Something Wicked This Way Comes	Rural Illinois, 1930s
All of Me	Los Angeles, 1980s
Crimes of Passion	An American city, 1980s
The Coca-Cola Kid	Sydney, Australia, 1980s
Kiss of the Spider Woman	A jail cell in South America, 1980s
Kiss of the Spider Woman	A jail cell in South America, 1980s
Broadcast News	Washington, D.C., 1980s

Character	Genre	Age	Page
Will Halloway A man remembering his past.	D	30-40	52
Roger/Edwina A hapless attorney forced to share his body with the soul of a bitchy female client.	C	30-40	55
Rev. Peter Shane A psychotic man obsessed with saving the soul of a prostitute.	SC	30-40	57
Becker An ex-Marine now employed as a trouble-shooter by the Cola-Cola company.	SC	30-40	64
Molina A man imprisoned for his homosexuality who keeps his spirits up by telling the story of his favorite movie.	D	30-40	68
Valentin Molina's cellmate; a man imprisoned for his politics.	D	30-40	68
Aaron A television journalist with integrity.	SC	30-40	95

Film	Setting
Fatal Attraction	NYC, 1980s
The Witches of Eastwick	A small New England town, 1980s
The Bird Man of Alcatraz	Alcatraz Prison
Tucker: The Man and His Dream	A U.S. courtroom, 1945
Mississippi Burning	Mississippi, 1964
Anne of the Thousand Days	The court of Henry VIII
Reuben, Reuben	A small town in New England, 1980s

Character	Genre	Age	Page
Dan A successful attorney seduced by a psychotic woman.	D	30-40	97
Darryl Van Horn A mysterious man with supernatural powers. (2 monologues)	SC	30-50	115, 117
Gomez A man sentenced to life in prison.	SC	30-50	8
Tucker An American visionary and inventor.	D	40s	123
Rupert An FBI agent raised in the south.	D	40s	126
Henry VIII Tempestuous king ruled by his lust for women.	D	40s	24
Gowan McGland A narcissistic poet wallowing in self-pity. (2 monologues)	SC	40s	149

Film	Setting
Desert Bloom	Las Vegas, 1950
Hannah and Her Sisters	Manhattan, 1980s
Hannah and Her Sisters	Manhattan, 1980s
The Mosquito Coast	Central America, 1980s
River's Edge	Oregon, 1980s
Salvador	El Salvador, 1980-82
Jaws	Amity Island, 1975

Character	Genre	Age	Page
Jack A WWII vet frustrated by his failures in life. (2 monologues)	SC	40s	76, 77
Elliot A NYC businessman facing a midlife crisis.	SC	40s	79
Mickey A TV executive with a touch of hypochondria.	SC	40s	79
Allie An eccentric inventor disenchanted with the American dream. (2 monologues)	D	40s	82
Feck A biker on the lam.	D	40s	89
Major Max A brutal military leader.	D	40s	92
Quint A salty old sea captain turned shark hunter.	D	40-50	29

Film	*Setting*
Under the Volcano	A Red Cross Ball in Mexico, late 1930s
Salvador	El Salvador, 1980-82
Full Metal Jacket	Parris Island Marine Base, 1968
Orphans	Newark, New Jersey, 1980s
The Bird Man of Alcatraz	Alcatraz Prison
Tucker: The Man and His Dream	Chicago, 1945
Something Wicked This Way Comes	Rural Illinois, 1930s

Character	Genre	Age	Page
Geoffrey Firmin Alchoholic ex-British Consul to Mexico living in despair.	SC	40-50	60
Archbishop Romero An outspoken clergyman martyred in El Salvador.	D	40-50	93
Sgt. Hartman A tough marine drill sergeant.	SC	40-50	101
Harold A big-time mobster with a soft spot for needy orphans.	SC	40-50	109
Robert Stroud A hostile and violent man transformed by his love for birds.	D	40-50	9
Abe Tucker's friend and business partner.	D	50-60	123
Mr. Halloway An older man plagued by feelings of guilt and inadequacy.	D	50-60	53

Film	*Setting*

WOMEN

Salome's Last Dance	A brothel in Victorian London
The Accused	A courtroom, 1980s
sex, lies, and videotape	Baton Rouge, La., the present
Butterfield 8	NYC, early 1960s
Of Human Bondage	Victorian England
Anne of the Thousand Days	The court of Henry VIII
King of Comedy	NYC, 1982

Character	Genre	Age	Page
Salome A young prostitute portraying Salome in Oscar Wilde's play.	D	18-20	111
Sarah A young woman gang raped in a bar.	D	20s	128
Ann An angry young wife.	D	20s	134
Gloria A promiscuous young model who has fallen in love for the first time. (2 monologues)	D	20-30	4, 5
Mildred Rogers A proud woman ruled by passion and determined to be free.	D	20-30	20
Anne Boleyn The proud and passionate wife of Henry VIII, whose inability to bear a son led to her doom.	D	20-30	25
Marsha An overzealous fan of a TV talk show host.	SC	20-30	41

Film	Setting
Nadine	A roadside saloon in Texas, 1954
The Days of Wine and Roses	San Francisco, early 1960s
When Harry Met Sally	NYC, the present
The Haunting	A haunted house in New England, early 1960s
Butterfield 8	NYC, early 1960s
All of Me	Los Angeles, 1980s
Out of Africa	Kenya, after 1914

Character	Genre	Age	Page
Renee A ditzy secretary with an axe to grind.	SC	20-30	107
Kirstie Clay An alchoholic young mother.	D	30s	11
Sally A professional woman looking for love.	SC	30s	132
Eleanor A woman with psychic ability who is driven to the edge by feelings of guilt. (3 monologues)	D	30-40	17, 18
Happy A failed chorus girl who now runs a brothel.	D	30-40	4
Roger/Edwina The soul of a miserable wealthy woman which has been accidentally transferred into the body of her attorney.	C	30-40	55
Karen A woman who finds love and passion in colonial Africa. (4 monologues)	D	30-40	71, 72

Film	Setting
Desert Bloom	Las Vegas, 1950
Hannah and Her Sisters	Manhattan, 1980s
Moonstruck	Brooklyn, 1980s
Bull Durham	Durham, N.C., 1980s
Mississippi Burning	Mississippi, 1964
The Witches of Eastwick	A small town in New England, 1980s
The Manchurian Candidate	The U.S., just after the Korean War, 1952

Character	Genre	Age	Page
Rose A woman remembering her coming of age in Las Vegas.	SC	30-40	76
Holly The turbulent middle sister frustrated by her failure as an actress.	SC	30-40	79
Loretta A beautiful widow on the verge of marrying a man she doesn't love.	SC	30-40	105
Annie Savoy A sexy school teacher who devotes her free time to the local baseball team.	SC	30-40	119
Mrs. Pell The long-suffering wife of a racist deputy.	D	30-40	126
Alex A woman with earthy appeal and supernatural powers.	SC	30-40	116
Mrs. Iselin This malefic woman is a Communist spy.	D	40-50	14

Film	Setting
Harold and Maude	The American Southwest, early 1970s
The Whales of August	Coastal Maine, 1980s

Character	Genre	Age	Page
Mrs. Chasen A silly society matron obsessed with finding a wife for her son.	C	40-50	27
Sarah An elderly widow remembering her husband on their anniversary.	D	60+	114

Acknowledgments

Grateful acknowledgment is made to the following for permission to reprint excerpts from screenplays:

ALCOY FILM INVESTMENT, LTD.
One monologue from *The Coca-Cola Kid*, screenplay by Frank Moorhouse and produced by David Roe. © Alcoy Film Investment, Ltd.

ALIVE FILMS
One monologue from *The Whales of August*, screenplay by David Berry. Copyright Alive Films.

WOODY ALLEN
Three monologues from *Hannah and Her Sisters* by Woody Allen. © 1986 by Orion Pictures Corporation. All rights reserved.

CASTLE ROCK ENTERTAINMENT, NORA EPHRON AND ALFRED A. KNOPF, INC.
Two monologues from *When Harry Met Sally*, written by Nora Ephron, produced by Rob Reiner and Andrew Scheinman, directed by Rob Reiner. Copyright © 1989, 1990 by Castle Rock Entertainment. All rights reserved.

CHARTWELL PARTNERS AND WARNER BROS. INC.
One monologue from *Blade Runner*. Copyright belongs exclusively to The Blade Runner Partnership. Copyright © 1982 by The Blade Runner Partnership.

COLUMBIA PICTURES INDUSTRIES, INC.
One monologue from *And Justice for All*, written by Barry Levinson and Valerie Curtin. Copyright © 1979 by Columbia Pictures Industries, Inc. All rights reserved. Reprinted by permission of Columbia Pictures Industries, Inc., Barry Levinson and Valerie Curtin. Three monologues from *Desert Bloom*, written by Eugene Corr. Copyright © 1985 by Columbia Pictures Industries, Inc. All rights reserved. Reprinted by permission of Columbia Pictures Industries, Inc. and Eugene Corr. One monologue from *Taxi Driver*, written by Paul Schrader. Copyright © 1976 by Columbia Pictures Industries, Inc. All rights reserved. Reprinted by permission of Columbia Pictures Industries, Inc. and Paul Schrader.

THE WALT DISNEY COMPANY
Two monologues from *Something Wicked This Way Comes*. © The Walt
Disney Company.

EMBASSY FILMS ASSOCIATES
One monologue from *The Sure Thing* by Steven L. Broom and Jonathan
Roberts, produced by Roger Birnbaum. Copyright © Embassy Films Associates.

PHYLLIS E. GADDIS AND MARJORIE TUOMI
Two monologues based on the book *The Birdman of Alcatraz* by Thomas E.
Gaddis. Copyright © 1983 by Thomas E. Gaddis.

HARPERCOLLINS PUBLISHERS, FABER AND FABER LTD., AND
CHARLOTTE SHEEDY LITERARY AGENCY, INC.
Two monologues from *Sex, Lies and Videotape* by Stephen Soderbergh.
Copyright © 1990 by Stephen Soderbergh. Reprinted by permission of
HarperCollins Publishers, Faber and Faber, Ltd., and Charlotte Sheedy Literary Agency, Inc.

HEMDALE FILM CORPORATION AND NEAL JIMENEZ
Three momologues from the screenplay of *The Rivers's Edge* by Neal Jimenez. Copyright © 1987 by Hemdale Film Corporation.

KINGS ROAD ENTERTAINMENT
One monologue from the screenplay of *Creator*. Reprinted by permission of
Kings Road Entertainment.

ALFRED A. KNOPF, INC., ANDRE DEUTSCH LTD., AND WARNER BROS.
INC.
Three monologues from *The Witches of Eastwick* by John Updike. Copyright
© 1984 by John Updike. Screenplay copyright © 1987 by Warner Bros. Inc.
Reprinted by permission of Alfred A. Knopf, Inc., Andre Deutsch Ltd., and
Warner Bros. Inc.

LUCASFILM LTD. (LFL)
Two monologues from *Tucker: The Man and His Dream*. Copyright © 1988
by Lucasfilm Ltd. (LFL). All rights reserved. Courtesy of Lucasfilm Ltd.

MCA PUBLISHING RIGHTS
Monologues from *All of Me*, *Anne of 1,000 Days*, *Under the Volcano*, *Repo
Man*, *The Last Temptation of Christ*, *Out of Africa*, and *Jaws*. Copyright © by
Universal Pictures, a Division of Universal City Studios, Inc. Courtesy of
MCA Publishing Rights, a Division of MCA Inc.

MGM/UA COMMUNICATIONS CO.

One monologue from *Coming Home*. Copyright © 1978 by United Artists Corporation. All rights reserved. Two monologues from *Moonstruck*. Copyright © 1987 by Metro-Goldwyn-Mayer Pictures, Inc. All rights reserved.

NATANT PRODUCTIONS, N.V. AND WARNER BROS. INC.

Two monologues from *Full Metal Jacket*. Copyright © 1987 by Warner Bros. Inc.

ORION PICTURES CORPORATION

Two monologues from *Mississippi Burning*, written by Chris Gerolmo. Copyright © 1989 by Orion Pictures Corporation. All rights reserved. One monologue from *Bull Durham*. Copyright © 1988 by Orion Pictures Corporation. All rights reserved.

PARAMOUNT PICTURES CORPORATION

Monologues from: *The Accused* Copyright © 1988 by Paramount Pictures Corporation. All rights reserved; *Fatal Attraction* Copyright © 1987 by Paramount Pictures Corporation. All rights reserved; *Ferris Bueller's Day Off* Copyright © 1986 by Paramount Pictures Corporation. All rights reserved; *Harold and Maude* Copyright © 1971 by Paramount Pictures Corporation and Mildred Lewis and Colin Higgins Productions, Inc. All rights reserved; *Nate and Hayes* Copyright © 1983 by Paramount Pictures Corporation. All rights reserved.

LEONARD SCHRADER

Two monologues from *Kiss of the Spider Woman*, screenplay by Leonard Schrader.

OLIVER STONE AND IXTLAN CORPORATION

Four monologues from *Platoon*, written by Oliver Stone. Copyright © 1986 by Oliver Stone. Two monologues from *Salvador*, written by Oliver Stone and Richard Boyle. Copyright © 1985 by Oliver Stone.

TRANS ATLANTIC PICTURES

One monologue from *Crimes of Pasion* by Barry Sandler.

TRI-STAR PICTURES, INC.

One monologue *Nadine* by Robert Benton. Copyright © 1987 by Tri-Star Pictures, Inc. One monologue from BIRDY by Sandy Kroopf and Jack Behr. Copyright © 1984 by Tri-Star Pictures, Inc.